March of America Fac

Navigations to Newe F

Jacque

Navigations
to Newe Fraunce

by Jacques Cartier
Translated by John Florio

ANN ARBOR

UNIVERSITY MICROFILMS, INC.

A Subsidiary of Xerox Corporation

Foreword

A Shorte And briefe narration of the two Navigations and Discoveries to the Northweast partes called Newe Fraunce provides an account of two voyages undertaken by the French navigator, Jacques Cartier, in search of a northern passage to the Orient. His discovery and exploration of the St. Lawrence River supplied France with a claim to this region in the New World. Cartier's voyages prepared the way for the penetration of French influence into North America and for the establishment of New France.

Cartier sailed on his first voyage to North America in 1534 under commission of King Francis I. At what is now Cape Gaspé, Cartier and his men landed and formally took possession of the territory for France. Cartier described how they "caused a fair high Crosse to be made," attached to which was a shield with three fleur de lys and an inscription "VIVE LE ROY DE FRANCE."

On the second voyage of 1535, Cartier discovered the St. Lawrence River and ascended it to a point near what is today the city of Montreal. Cartier and his men were favorably impressed by the country, "as fayre and as pleasaunte as possiblye can bee seene, being leavell, smoothe, and very playne, fitte to be husbanded and tilled." However the expedition took greater interest in the tantalizing reports of "infinite Rubies, Golde, and other riches" which, so the Indians told them, lay beyond in the interior. Before returning to France Cartier determined to "playe a pretty prancke." He kidnapped the local Indian chief and several of the principal men of the tribe so that he might present them for interrogation by the King of France.

A third voyage which Cartier made to Canada in 1541 to help establish a colony there is not described in this edition. The attempt at colonization ended in failure, and for a variety of reasons the French temporarily lost interest.

The narrations of the first two voyages may have been expansions by Cartier of material contained in the ship's log, though there is some dispute about this. In any event an Italian, Giovanni Ramusio, obtained copies of these two narrations from friends in Paris and published them in an Italian translation in 1556. John Florio, encouraged by Richard Hakluyt the younger, then published his English translation from the Italian in 1580. Florio hoped that knowledge of Cartier's voyages "might suffice to induce oure Englishmen not only to fall in some traffic with the Inhabitants, but also to plant a colony in some convenient place and to possess the country." Additional information about these accounts of Cartier's voyages can be found in Henry P. Bigger's edition of *The Voyages of Jacques Cartier* (Ottawa, 1924), pp. ix-xiv, and in Bernard G. Hoffman, *Cabot to Cartier* (Toronto, 1961), pp. 131-167.

Navigations to Newe Fraunce

¶A SHORTE AND
briefe narration of the two
Nauigations and Discoueries
to the Northweast partes called
NEWE FRAVNCE:

First translated out of French into Italian, by that famous
learned man *Gio : Bapt : Ramutius*, and now turned
into English by *Iohn Florio :* Worthy the rea-
ding of all Venturers, Trauellers,
and Discouerers.

IMPRINTED AT LON-
don, by H. Bynneman, dvvelling
in Thames streate, neere vnto
Baynardes Castell.

Anno Domini. 1 5 8 0.

¶TO THE RIGHT VVOR-
ſhipful Edmond Bray Eſquire, High
Sherife within hir Maieſties Countie
of Oxenford: I. Florio vviſheth much
encreaſe of worſhip in this life, and in
the Worlde to come, eternall
happineſſe.

He olde ſaying is : None ſo bolde as blynd Bayard:
nor anye ſo readye to vndertake, as the leaſte able
to performe : Euen ſo (right Worſhipfull) it nowe
fareth with me, who (at the requeſts and earneſte
ſolicitations of diuers my very good frends heere in
Oxforde) haue vndertaken this tranſlation, wher-
in I holde my ſelfe farre inferiour to many. Howbeeit, foraſmuch as
that ſeruaunt was of his Lord and Maiſter moſt highly diſcommen-
ded, whiche hiding his Talent in the grounde , had thereby profited
nothing: my ſelfe being very loath to incurre the ſame faulte, and ſo
to become worthy the like reprehenſion, haue the rather aduentured
to tranſlate this parte of Nauigation, whiche (I aſſure my ſelfe with
other mens trauel and diligence) may be an occaſion of no ſmal commoditie and benefite to this our Countrie of Englande. And heerein
the more to animate and encourage the Engliſhe Marchants , I doe
onely (for breuitie ſake) propoſe vnto them the infinite treaſures (not
hidden to themſelues) whiche both the Spaniardes, the Portugales,
and the Venetians haue ſeuerally gained by their ſuche nauigations
and trauailes. Nowe (right Worſhipful) when I had well conſidered
with my ſelfe, that hir Maieſtie hathe deemed your Worſhip a very
meete man for that auctloritie wherein you nowe preſently remaine,
I my ſelfe coulde not but accompt your Worſhip (for the preſent) the
fitteſt man within the ſhire, to patronize and defende this my ſimple
labour, whereby any benefite maye either happen to hir Maieſties
perſon, or commoditie , to hir highneſſe common weale : and if the
wealthe of a Prince be any cauſe of the ſafetie of his perſon, (which,
who doubteth? it may be (and not vntruly) ſaide to be bothe. But to
the ende your Worſhippe haue not altogither ſo muche cauſe to con-

A.ij.   demne

The Epistle Dedicatorie:

demne me for this my bolde attempt vpon no maner of acquaintance,
I thought it not vnfit vnto you, that I haue the rather herevnto pre-
sumed, vppon the request and warrant of my deare and welbeloued
friend Maister H. Leigh, who (no doubt) is a man verie mindfull
of al your Worships. courtesies from time to time shewed toward him.
Thus not willingly desirous to be herein more tedious than is re-
quisite, I cease from troubling your good Worship, hartily praying
the Almightie, to encrease the same, with abundaunce of
all other vertues, to his good wil and pleasure: and
withall, wholly committe my selfe vnto
your Worships good disposition.
From Oxenford the 25.
of Iune. 1 5 8 0.
(∵)

Your Worships most humble at
commaundement. I. Florio.

¶ To all Gentlemen, Merchants,
and Pilots.

Hen I had taken in hande to tranflate thys Treatife, which I did for the benefite and behoofe of thofe that fhall attempt any newe difcouerie in the Northweaft partes of *America*, I thought good brieflye to touch the vfe of my tranflation, that the Reader may fee and confider the drift of my trauell. For, although this Difcourfe may feeme very barraine, and not to containe fuche matter as is pretended, as beyng a particular Relation of certaine Prouinces whyche haue beene hitherto of all men rather contemned than throughly knowen : yet if the Marchant Venturer, or skilfull Pilot, or whofoeuer defirous of newe Difcoueries, haue the readyng and perufing thereof, for whome efpecially I haue done it into Englifhe, they will find matter worthy the looking, and confequently, gratefully accept my paines herein. For here is the Defcription of a Countrey no leffe fruitful and pleafant in al refpects than is *England*, *Fraunce*, or *Germany*, the people, though fimple and rude in manners, and deftitute of the knowledge of God or any good lawes, yet of nature gentle and tractable, and moft apt to receiue the Chriftian Religion, and to fubiect themfelues to fome good gouernement : the commodities of the Countrey not inferiour to the Marchandize of *Mofcouy*, *Danske*, or many other frequented trades : the voyage verye fhorte, being but three weekes fayling from *Briftowe*, *Plymmouth*, or any commodious Porte of the Weaft Country, with

a direct courſe to the coaſt of the Newe found land. Al which
oportunities beſides manye others, mighte ſuffice to induce
oure Engliſhemen, not onely to fall to ſome traffique wyth
the Inhabitants, but alſo to plant a Colonie in ſome conuenient place, and ſo to poſſeſſe the Countrey without the gain-
ſaying of any man, whiche was the iudgement and counſell
of *Iohn Baptiſta Ramuſius*, a learned and excellent Coſmogra-
pher, & Secretary to the famous ſtate of *Venice*, whoſe words,
bicauſe they are not impertinēt to this purpoſe, I haue here ſet
downe. Why doe not the Princes (ſaieth he) whyche are to
deale in theſe affaires, ſende forth two or three Colonies to inhabite the Country, & to reduce this ſauage natiō to ſome ciuilitie? conſidering what a battle and fruitfull ſoyle it is, how
repleniſhed with all kinde of graine, how it is ſtored wyth al
ſortes of Byrdes and Beaſtes, wyth ſuch faire and mighty Riuers, that Captaine *Carthier* and his company, in one of them
ſayled vppe a hundreth and foure ſcore leagues, findyng the
countrey peopled on both ſides in greate abundaunce. And
moreouer, to cauſe the Gouernors of thoſe Colonies to ſend
forth men to ſearch and diſcouer the North lands about *Ter-
ra del Lauorader*, and toward Weaſt northweaſt to the Seas
whiche are to ſaile to the Country of *Cataya*, and from thence
to the Ilands of *Molucke*. Theſe were enterpriſes to purchaſe
immortall praiſe, which the Lord *Anthony di Mendoza* Vice-
roy of *Mexico*, willing to put in execution, ſent forth his Cap-
tains both by Sea and by Land vpon the Northweaſt of *Nuo-
ua Spagona*, and diſcouered the Kingdome of the ſeauen Cities
about *Ciuola*. And *Franciſcus Vaſques de Coronada*, paſſed from
Mexico by ſande towarde the Northweaſt 2850. miles, in ſo
muche, that he came to the Sea, whyche lyeth betweene *Cataya* and *America*, where he met with the Catayan ſhyppes.
And no doubt, if the French men in this their newe *Fraunce*,
would haue diſcouered vp further into the land towards the
Weaſt northweaſt partes, they ſhoulde haue founde the Sea,
and might haue ſayled to *Cataya*. Thus much out of *Ramuſius*, where you may ſee this learned mans iudgement concerning

cerning the planting of Colonies, and inhabiting these countries, whych might be a meane, not only to discouer the Sea
on the backe-side, as he desireth, but also to come vnto the
knowledge of the Countries adiacent: and namely, of *Sague-*
nay, whiche aboundeth with Golde and other Mettalles, as in
the seconde Relation is to be seene. All whyche thyngs, excepte they builde and inhabite, can neuer be atchieued, for as
Fraunciscus Lopez di Gomara, and dyuers other Spanishe Au-
thors affirme, the Spanyards neuer prospered or preuailed,
but where they planted: whych of the Portingales maye also be verifyed, as in the Histories of all theyr Conquests and
Discoueries doth manifestly appeare. And as there is none,
that of right may be more bolde in this enterprice than the
Englishmen, the land being first found out by *Iohn Gabot* the
Father, and *Sebastian Gabot*, one of hys three sonnes, in the
yeare 1494. in the name and behalfe of King *Henry* the seauenth, as both by the foresaide *Ramusius* in his first Volumes,
and our owne Chronicles, and *Sebastian Gabots* letters pa-
tents yet extant, and in his Mappe maye be seene: so there is
no nation that hath so good righte, or is more fit for this purpose, than they are, who trauayling yearely into those partes
with 50. or 60. saile of shippes, might very commodiouslye
transporte a sufficient number of men to plant a Colonie in
some conuenient Hauen, and also might yeeld them yearly
succour, and supply of al things necessary, receyuing againe
such commodities as the country doth produce. And this the
Frenchmen had done long since, if first their warres with the
Spanyardes, and since their cruell dissentions at home, had
not hindered them. And *Iohannes Varrozzana* a Florentine, if
he had not beene preuented by death, purposed (as the fore-
sayde *Ramusius* writeth) to perswade *Francis* the French King
to send forth good store of people to inhabite certaine places
of these coastes, where the aire is moste temperate, and the
soyle moste fruitfull, with goodly Riuers and Hauens sufficient to harborough any nauie, the inhabitantes of which places might be occasiō to bring many good purposes to effecte,

and

and amongest manye others, to reduce those poore rude and ignorant people to the true worship and seruice of God, and to teache them how to manure and till the ground, transporting ouer Beastes and Cattell of *Europe* into those large and champion countreys, and finally, in time they might discouer vp into the land, and search, whether among so many Ilands as are there, there be any passage to the Sea of *Cataya*. And thus much oute of the third Volume of Voyages and Nauigations, gathered into the Italian tongue by *Ramusius*: whiche Bookes, if they were translated into English by the liberalitie of some noble Personage, our Sea-men of *England*, and others, studious of Geographie, shoulde know many worthy secrets, whiche hitherto haue beene concealed. For, the beste Cosmographers of this age (as I am by the skilfull in those Sciences informed, and as to him that doth diligently consider their Mappes, it shall plainely appeare) haue described *Asia*, *Africa*, and *America*, chiefly by the help of those bookes. But to returne to that from whence I did digresse, althoughe some attemptes of oure Countrey-men haue not had as yet suche successe as was wished, they ought not therefore to bee the slower in this enterprice, for if they were of late contented in their voyage, to haue stayed al the Winter in those colder Countries, if their store of victualles had beene sufficient, howe muche rather ought we nowe in a farre more temperate clime, where *Iames Carthier*, accompanyed wyth 1 2 0. men remained a whole Winter contrary to hys determination when he set out of *Fraunce*? Thus beseeching God, that this my trauel may take that effect for the which it is meant, I commende the diligent consideration to al such Gentlemen, Merchants, and Pilots, as seeke Gods glory, the aduauncement of their Countrey, and the happy successe, to the prouidence of the Almighty, who in my opinion hath not in vaine stirred vppe the mindes of so many Honourable and Worshipfull persons to the furtheraunce of these commendable and worthy Discoueries.

In Oxford, *I. F.*

¶ The first relation of Iames Carthier of the new land called New Fraunce, nevvly discouered in the yeare of oure Lorde, 1534.

¶ How Maister Iames Carthier departed from the Port of *S. Malo*, with two Ships, and came to the new land, and howe he entred into the Porte of *Buona Vista*.

Fter that Sir Charles of *Mouy*, knight, Lord of *Meyleray*, & Vice-admirall of *Fraunce*, had caused all the Captaines, Maisters, and Mariners of the Shippes to be sworne to behaue themselues truely and faithfully in the seruice of the most Christian King of *France*, vnder the charge of the sayde Carthier, vpon the 20. day of Aprill. 1534. we departed from the Porte of *S. Malo* with two Ships of thre score tun apeece burden, and by well appointed men in eche one, and with suche prosperous weather, we sailed onwardes, that vppon the 10. of May we came to the newe found land, where we entred into the cape of *Buona Vista*, which is in Latitude 48. degrees and a halfe, and in Longitude. ✳. But bicause of the great store of Ice that was alongest the sayde lande, we were constrayned to enter into a Hauen called, Saint Katherins Hauen, distaunt from the other Porte aboute fiue leagues towarde South southeast: there did we stay ten daies, loking for faire weather, and in the meane while we mended and dressed our boates.

C¶   How

The first Relation.

¶ Howe we came to the Ilande of Byrdes, and of the greate quantitie of Byrdes that there be.

Vpon the 21. of May the wind beyng in the Weast, we hoised saile, and sailed toward North and by east from ye Cape of *Buona Vista* vntil we came to the Iland of Birdes, which was enuironed about with a banke of Ice, but broke and crackte. Notwithstanding the saide banke, our two boates went thither to take in some Birdes, whereof there is such plentie, that vnlesse a manne didde see them, he woulde think it an incredible thing; for albeit the Ilande (which containeth aboute a league in circuite) be so full of them, that they seeme to haue beene brought thither, and sowed for the nonce, yet are there a hundreth fold as many houering about it as within, some of the which are as big as Iayes, blacke and white, with beakes lyke vnto Crowes: they houer alwaies about the sea, they cannot flye very high, bycause their wings are so little, and no bigger than halfe ones hand, yet doe they flye as swiftly as any birdes of the ayre leuell to the water, they are also exceeding fat: we named them Aporath. In lesse than halfe an houre we filled two boats ful of them, as if they had beene with stones : so that besides them which we did eate fresh, euery ship dyd powder and salt fiue or sixe barrels ful of them.

¶ Of two sortes of Byrdes, the one called *Godetz*, the other *Margaulz :* and how we came to *Carpunt.*

Besides these, there is an other kinde of Birdes, whyche houer in the aire ouer the sea, lesser than the others: and these doe al gather theselues togither in the Iland, & put theselues vnder the wings of other byrds that are greater: these we named Godetz. There are also of another sorte, but bigger, & white, who bite euen as Dogges : those wee named Margaulz. And albeit the said Ilande be 14. leagues from the maine lande, notwithstanding Beares come swimming thither

thither to eaſe of the ſaide Byrdes : and our men founde one
there as greate as any Cowe, and as white as any Swanne,
who in their preſence leapt into the ſea, and vpon Whitſon-
monday (folowing our voyage towarde the lande) we mette
hir by the way, ſwimming towarde lande as ſwiftly as wée
coulde ſaile : ſo ſoone as we ſawe hir we purſued hir with our
boates, and by maine ſtrength tooke hir, whoſe fleſh was as
good to be eaten, as the fleſhe of a Calfe of two yeares olde.
The Wedneſday following beyng the 27. of the moneth, we
came to the entrance of the Bay of the Caſtels, but bycauſe
the weather was ill, and the greate ſtore of Ice wée founde,
we were conſtrayned to enter into an harborough about the
ſaide entraunce called _Carpunt_, where, bycauſe wée could not
come oute of it, we ſtayed till the 9. of June, that thence wée
departed, on hope with the aide of God to ſaile further than
the ſaid _Carpunt_, which is in latitude 51. degrées.

¶ The deſcription of the newe founde lande, from Cape
Razo, to the Cape of _Degrade_.

The lande from Cape _Razo_, to the Cape of _Degrade_, whiche is the point of the entrance to the Bay that trendeth
from head to head toward North northeſt, and South ſouthweaſt, al this part of land is parted into Ilands, one ſo néere
the other, that there are but ſmall riuers betwéene them, tho-
rowe the whyche you may paſſe with little boates, and therfore there are certaine good harbourghs, among whyche is
that of _Carpunt_, and that of _Degrade_. In one of theſe Ilands,
that is the higheſt of them all, béyng on the toppe of it,
you maye playnely ſée the two lowe Ilandes, that are
neare to Cape _Razo_, from whence to the Porte of _Carpunt_,
they counte it twentie and fiue leagues, and there are two
entraunces thereat, one on the Eaſt, the other on the South
ſide of the Iland. But it is to be noted, that from the ſide,
and pointe of the Eaſte, bycauſe that euerye where
C.y.   there

there is nothing elſe but ſhelues, and the water is very ſhal-
lowe : you muſte goe aboute the Ilande towarde the Weſt
the length of halfe a Cable or thereaboute, and then to goe
towarde the South, to the ſaid *Carpont*. Alſo you are to take
héede of thrée Shelues that are in the Chanel vnder the water: and towarde the Iland on the Eaſte ſide in the Chanell,
the water is about two faddome déepe, and cleare grounde.
The other trendeth toward Eaſt northeaſt, and on the Weſt
you may go on ſhoare.

¶ Of the Ilande whiche now is called Saint
Katherins Ilande.

GOing from the Point of *Degrade*, and entring into the
ſayde Baye towarde the Weaſt, and by North: there is
ſome doubt of two Ilandes that are on the right ſide, one of
the whiche is diſtant from the ſaide pointe 3.leagues, and the
other 7. either more or leſſe than the firſt, beyng a lowe and
plaine land, and it ſéemeth to be parte of the maine lande. I
named it Saint Katherines Ilande : inwhich, toward North-
eaſt there is verye drye ſoile : but aboute a quarter of a league from it, very ill ground, ſo that you muſte goe a little a-
bout. The ſaide Iland, and the Porte of Caſtelles trend towarde North northeaſt, and South ſouthweaſt, and they are
about 15. leagues aſunder. From the ſaide Porte of Caſtels
to the Porte of *Gutte*, whyche is in the northerne parte of the
ſaid Bay, that trendeth towarde Eaſt northeaſt, and Weaſt
ſouthweaſt, there are twelue leagues and an halfe : and a-
boute two leagues from the Porte of *Balances*, that is to ſay,
the thirde parte, athwarteth the ſayde Bay : the deapth being ſounded it is about 18.faddomes: and from the ſaid Porte
of *Balances* to the White Sands toward Weaſt ſouthweaſt
there is 15. leagues, but you muſt take héede of a ſhelfe that
lyeth about 3.leagues outward from the ſayd White Sands
on the Southweaſt ſide aboue water like a Boate.

Of

¶ Of the place called *White Sandes*: of the Ilande of *Breſt*, and of the Ilande of Byrdes : the ſortes and quantitie of Byrdes that there are founde: and of the Porte called the *Iſlettes*.

Hite *Sandes* is a Roade in the whiche there is no place garded from the South, nor Southeaſt. But towarde South southweaſt the ſaid roade there are two Ilandes, one of the which is called *Breſt* Iland, and the other the Ilande of Byrdes, in whiche there is great ſtore of Godetz, & Crowes with red beakes and redde féete: they make their néſtes in holes vnder the ground euen as Connies. A point of land being paſſed about a league from *White Sands*, there is a Port & paſſage found, called the *Iſlettes*, a better place than *White Sandes*: and there is great fiſhing. From the ſaide Porte of the *Iſlettes*, vnto another called *Breſt* : the circuite is aboute ten leagues. This Porte is in latitude 51. degrées and 55. minutes, and in longitude. *. From the *Iſlettes*, to that place there are many other Ilandes: and the ſaide Porte of *Breſt* is alſo amongſt thoſe Ilandes. Moreouer the Ilands doe compaſſe more than 3. leagues from the ſaid *Breſt*, beyng lowe, and ouer them are the other landes (aboue mentioned) féene.

¶ Howe we wyth our Shippes entred into the Porte of *Breſt*, and ſayling onwarde towarde the Weaſt, we paſt amidſt the *Iſlettes*, which were ſo many in number, that it was not poſſible to tel them: and how we named thē the *Iſlettes*.

Pon the 10. of Iune we with our Ships entred into the Port of *Breſt*, to furniſh our ſelues with water and wood, and to make vs readye to paſſe the ſaide Bay. Upon Saynt Barnabas day, ſeruice being heard, we with our boates went beyond the ſaid Porte toward the Weaſt, to ſée what harboroughes were there: we paſſed throughe the middeſt of the

Iſlettes, which were ſo many in number, that it was not poſſible they might be told, for they continued about 10. leagues
beyonde the ſaide Porte. We to reſt our ſelues ſtayed in one
of them a night, and there we found greate ſtore of Ducke
egges, and other byrdes that there doe make their neaſtes,
we named them all, the Iſlettes.

¶ Of the Porte called S. Antonies Porte, S. Seruans Porte,
Iames Carthiers Porte: of the riuer called S. Iames: of the
cuſtomes and apparell of the inhabitors in the Iland of
White Sandes.

THe next day we paſſed the ſaide Ilandes, and beyonde
them all we found a good Hauen, whyche we named S.
Antonies Hauen, and howe one or two leagues beyonde, we
founde a little riuer toward the Southweſt coaſt, that is betwéene two other Ilandes, and is a good harborough. There
we ſette vppe a Croſſe, and named it S. Seruans Porte : and
on the Southweſt ſide of the ſaid Porte and riuer, about one
league, there is a ſmall Ilande as round as any Ouen, enuironed about with many other little Ilandes, that giue notice
to the ſaide Portes. Further about two leagues, there is an
other greater riuer, in whiche they toke good ſtore of Sal-
mon, that we named S. Iames his Riuer. Beyng in the ſayde
riuer, we ſawe a Shippe of Rochell that the night before had
paſſed the Porte of Breſt, where they thought to haue gone a
fiſhing: but the marriners not knowing where they were, we
with our boates approched neare vnto it, and did directe it to
another Porte one league more toward the Weaſt than the
ſaide riuer of S. Iames, which I take to be one of the beſte in
all the Worlde, and therefore wée named it Iames Carthiers Sound. If the ſoile were as good as the harboroughes are,
it were a great commoditie: but it is not to be called the new
Land, but rather Stones, and wilde Furres, and a place ſitte
for wilde beaſtes, for in all the Northe Ilande I didde not
ſée a Cartloade of good earth: yet went I on ſhoare in many
places,

places, and in the Iland of White Sandes, there is nothyng else but Mosse, and small Thornes scattered here and there, withered and drye. To be shorte, I beléeue that this was the lande that God allotted to Caine. There are men of an indifferent good stature and bignesse, but wilde and vnruly: they weare their haire tyed on the top like a wreath of Hay, and put a wooden pin within it, or any other such thing, in steade of a naile, and wyth them they binde certaine birdes feathers. They are clothed with beastes skinnes, as wel the men as womē, but that the womē go somwhat straight-lier and closer in their garmentes than men doe, wyth their wastes gyrded: they paint themselues with certaine Roan coloures: their Boates are made of the barke of a trée cal-led *Boul*, wyth the whyche they fishe, and take greate store of Seales, and as farre as we coulde vnderstande since oure commyng thither, that is not their habitation, but they come from the maine lande out of hotter Countreys, to take of the sayde Seales and other necessaries for theyr ly-uing.

¶ Of certaine Capes, that is to say, the *double Cape*, the *poin-ted Cape*, *Cape Roiall*, and the *Cape of Milke*: of the *Moun-taines of Barnes*: of the Ilandes of *Doue houses*: and of the greate fishing of Cods.

Vpon the 13. of that moneth we came to our Shippes a-gayne with our boates, on purpose to saile forwards, by-cause the weather was faire, & vpon Sundaye we caused ser-uice to be saide: then on Monday being the 15. of the moneth, we departed from *Brest* and sailed toward the South to take a viewe of the landes that there we had séene, that séemed vnto vs to be two Ilandes: but when we were amiddest the Bay, we knew it to be firme lande, where was a greate double Cape, one aboue the other, and therfore wée named it the Double Cape. In the entrance of the Bay we sounded, and founde it to be an hundred faddome rounde aboute vs.

From

From *Breſt*, to the double Cape, there is about 20 leagues, and aboute fiue oz ſixe leagues beyond we ſounded againe, and founde 20 faddome water. The ſaide lande lyeth Noztheaſt, and Southweaſt. The nexte day being the 16. of the moneth, we ſailed along the ſaide coaſte towarde Southweaſt, and by South, aboute 35 leagues from the double Cape, where wée founde very ſtæpe and wilde hilles, among the whyche were ſéene certaine ſmall Cabbans, whyche we in the Countrey call Barnes, and therfoze we named them the Hilles of the Barnes. The other Lands and Mountaines are all craggie, cleft, and cutte, and betwixt them and the ſea, there are other Ilandes, but lowe. The day befoze, thzough the darke miſts and fogges of the weather, we coulde not haue ſighte of any lande , but in the euening we ſpyed an entraunce into the lande, by a ryuer, among the ſaide Hilles of Barnes , and a Cape lying towarde the Southweſt about 3. leagues frō vs. The ſaide Cape is on the top of it blunt pointed , and alſo towarde the Sea, it endeth in a pointe, wherefoze we named it the pointed Cape, on the nozth ſide of whiche , there is a plaine Iland. And bycauſe we would haue notice of the ſaid entrance, to ſée if there were any good Hauens, we ſtroke ſaile foz that night. The next day being the 17. of the Moneth, we had ſtozmie weather from Noztheaſt , wherefoze we tōke our way toward the Southweſt vntil Thurſeday mozning, and we went about 37. leagues, til we came athwart a Bay full of rounde Ilandes like Doue houſes, and therefoze wée named them the Doue houſes. And from the Bay of Saint *Iulian,* from the whyche to a Cape that lyeth South and by weaſt, which we called Cape Riall, there are 7. leagues, and toward the Weaſt Southweaſt ſide of the ſaide Cape there is another that beneath is all craggie, and aboue round. On the Nozth ſide of whiche about halfe a league there lyeth a lowe Iland, that Cape we named the Cape of Milke. Betwéene theſe two Capes there are certaine lowe Ilandes, aboue whiche, there are alſo certaine others, that ſhew that there be ſome riuers. About two leagues from Cape Roiall, wée

Capo Latte.

we founded, and found tenne faddome water, and there is the greateſt fiſhing of Coddes that is poſſible: for ſtaying for our companie, in leſſe than an houre we toke aboue an hundred of them.

¶ Of certayne Ilands that lie betweene Cape *Roiall*, and the Cape of *Milke*.

THe nexte daye, being the eyghtenth of the Moneth, the winde with ſuch rage turned againſt vs, that we were conſtrayned to go backe toward Cape Royall, thinking there to find ſome harborough, and with oure Boates wente to diſcouer betwéene the Cape Royall, and the Cape of Milke, and found, that aboue the low Ilands there is a great, and very déepe Gulſe, within which are certaine Ilands. The ſayd Gulſe on the South ſide is ſhutte vp. The foreſayd low grounds are on one of the ſides of the entrance, and Cape Royall is on the other. The ſayde lowe groundes do ſtretche themſelues more than halfe a league within the Sea. It is a playne Countrey, but an ill ſoyle: and in the middeſt of the entrance thereof, there is an Iland. The ſayde Gulſe in latitude is fortie eyght degrées and an halfe, and in Longitude. *. That night we found no harborough, and therefore we launched out into the Sea, leauing the Cape toward the Weaſt.

¶ Of the Iland called *S. Iohn.*

FRom the ſayde daye vntill the 24. of the moneth, being S. Iohns day, we had both ſtormie weather and winde againſt vs, with ſuch darkneſſe and miſtes, that vntill Saint Iohns day, we could haue no ſight of any land, and then had we ſight of a Cape of land, y̆ from Cape Royall lieth Southweaſt, about 35. leagues, but that day was ſo foggie and miſtie, that we could not come néere land, and bycauſe it was S. Iohns day, we named it Cape S. Iohn.

D.   ¶ Of

The first Relation.

¶ Of certayne Ilands called the Ilands of *Margaulz*, and of the kinds of beastes and birds that there are found. Of the Iland of *Brion*, and Cape *Dolphin*.

The nexte daye being the 25. of the moneth, the weather was also ſtormie, darke, and windie, but yet we ſayled a part of the day toward Weaſt North-weaſt, and in the euening we put our ſelues athwart vnto the ſecond quarter that thence we departed, then did we by our compaſſe know that we were North-weaſt, and by Weaſt about ſeauen leagues and an halfe from the Cape of S. Iohn, and as we were aboute to hoyſe ſayle, the wind turned into the North-weaſt, wherefore we went toward North-eaſt, about fifteene leagues, and came to three Ilands, two of whiche are as ſteepe and vpright as any wall, that it was not poſſible to climbe them: and betweene them there is a little clift. Theſe Ilands were as full of Birds, as any fielde or meddow is of graſſe, that there do make their neſtes: and in the greateſt of them, there was a great and infinite number of thoſe that we cal Margaulz, that are white, and bigger than any Geeſe, which were ſeuered in one part. In the other were only Godetz Iſoli, but towarde the ſhoare there were of thoſe Godetz; and greate Apponatz, like to thoſe of that Ilande that we aboue haue mentioned: we went downe to the loweſt part of the leaſt Iland, where we kild aboue a thouſand of thoſe Godetz, & Apponatz. We put into our Boates ſo many of them as wee pleaſed, for in leſſe than one houre, we might haue filled thirtie ſuch boates of them: we named them the Ilands of Margaultz. About fiue leagues from the ſayde Ilandes, on the Weaſt, there is another Iland that is about two leagues in length, and ſo much in breadth: there did we ſtay all night to take in water and wood. That Ilante is enuironed rounde about with ſande, and hath a very good roade about it three or four faddome deepe. Thoſe Ilands haue the beſt ſoyle that euer we ſaw, for that one of their feelds is more woorth, than all the new land. We foūd it all full of goodly trees, medowes,
cham-

rhampaines full of wild peason blomed, as thicke, as ranke, and as faire, as any can be séene in _Brittayne_, that they séemed to haue bin plowed and sowed. There was also great store of goseberies, strawberies, damaske roses, parseley, with other very swéete and pleasant hearbes. About the said Iland are very great beaftes, as great as Oren, which haue two great téeth in their mouths like vnto the Elephant, and liue also in the Sea. We saw one of them sléeping vpon the banke of the water : we thinking to take it, went to it with our Boates, but so soone as he heard vs, he cast himselfe into the Sea. We also sawe Beares, and Wolues : we named it Brions Iland. About it towarde South-eaft, and North-weaft, there are great medowes. As farre as I could gather and comprehend, I thinke that there be some passage betwéene the new land, and Brions land, if so it were, it would be a great shortning, as well of the time, as of the way, if any perfection coulde be founde in it. Aboute foure leagues from that Ilande to-warde Weft South-weaft, there is firme lande, that séemeth to be as an Ilande, compassed aboute with little Ilands of sandes. There is a goodly Cape, which we named Cape Doulphin, for there is the beginning of good groundes. On the seauen and twentith of _Iune_ we compassed the said landes about that lie Weaft South-weaft : a farre off they séeme to bée little hilles of sande, for they are but lowe landes : we coulde neyther goe to them, nor land on them, bycause the winde was against vs. That daye we wente fiftéene leagues.

¶ Of the Iland called _Alezai_. and of _S. Peeters_ Cape.

The next day we went along the said land aboute tenne leagues, till we came to a Cape of redde lands, that is all craggie, within the which, there is a bracke looking toward the North. It is a very low Countrey. There is also betwéene ỹ sea ҫ a certain poole a plaine field: and frõ that Cape of land and ỹ poole, vntill to another Cape, there is about 14 leagues.

The

The land is faſhioned as it were halfe a circle, all compaſſed about with ſand like a ditch, ouer which, as farre as ones eye can ſtretch, there is nothing but marriſh groundes, and ſtanding pooles. And before you come to the firſt Cape, very neere the mayne lande, there are two little Ilands. Aboute fiue leagues from the ſeconde Cape towarde South weaſt, there is another Iland very high and poynted, which we named Alezai. The firſt Cape we named S. Peeters Cape, bycauſe vpon that day we came thither.

¶ Of the Cape called *Orleans* Cape: of the Riuer of Boates: of wild mens Cape: and of the qualitie and temperature of the Countrey.

FRom Brions Iland to this place, there is a good ſandie ground, and hauing ſounded toward South weaſt euen to the Shoare, about fiue leagues, we found 12. faddome water, and within one league 6. and very neere the ſhoare rather more than leſſe. But bycauſe we would be better acquaynted with this ſtonie and rockie ground, we ſtroke our Sayles lowe and athwart. The nexte daye being the laſt of the moneth ſaue one, the winde blewe South and by Eaſt. We ſayled Weſtwarde vntill Tueſday morning at Sunne riſing, beeing the laſt of the moneth, without any ſighte or knowledge of any lande, except in the euening towarde Sunne ſette, that we diſcouered a Land, whiche ſeemed to bee two Ilandes, that were beyond vs Weſt ſouthweaſt, about nine or tenne leagues. All the next day till the nexte morning at Sunne riſing we ſayled Weſtward about fortye leagues, and by the way we perceyued that the lande wee hadde ſeene like two Ilandes, was firme lande, lying South ſouth-eaſt, and North north-weaſt, till to a verye good Cape of lande called Orleans Cape. All the ſayde lande is lowe and playne, and the faireſt that may poſſibly be ſeene, full of goodly meddowes and Trees. True it is that we could finde no harborough there, bycauſe it is

all

all full of shelues and sandes. We with our boates went on shore in many places, and among the reste we entred into a goodly riuer, but very shallow, which we named the riuer of boats, bycause that there we saw boats ful of wild men, that were crossing the riuer. We had no other notice of the sayde wilde men : for the winde came from the Sea, and beate vs againste the shore, that we were constrained to retire oure selues with our boates toward our shippes, till the next day morning at Sunne rising, being the firste of July, we sayled Northeast, in which time there rose great mystes & stormes, and therefore we strucke our sayles till two of the clocke in the after noone, that the weather became cleare, and there we had sight of Orleance Cape, & of another about seuē leagues from vs, lying North and by East, and that we called Wilde mens Cape. On the Northside of this Cape aboute halfe a league, there is a very dangerous shelf, and banke of stones. Whilest we wer at this Cape, we saw a man running after our boats that were going along the coast, who made signes vnto vs that we shoulde retourne towarde the sayd Cape againe We seeing such signes, began to tourne toward him, but he seeing vs come, began to flee : so soone as we were come on shoare, we set a knife before him, and a woollen girdle on a little staffe, and then came to our ships again. That day we trended the sayde land about nine or ten leagues, hoping to finde some good harborough, but it was not possible, for as I haue sayd alreadie, it is a very low land, & enuironed round about with great shelues. Neuerthelesse we went that day on shore in foure places to see the goodly and sweete smelling trees that there were: we founde them to be Cidrons, Ewe trees, Pines, white Elmes, Ashes, Willowes, with manye other sortes of trees to vs vnknowen, but without any fruit. The groundes where no wood is, are very faire, and al full of peason, white and red gooseberies, strawberies, blacke beries, and wilde corne, euen like vnto Rie, that it seemeth to haue bene sowen and plowed. This Countrey is of better temperature than any other that can be seene, and very hote.

There are many Thꝛuſhes, Stockdoues,and other byꝛdes: to be ſhoꝛt,there wanteth nothing but gꝺd harboꝛough.

¶ Of the Baie called *Saint Lunario* , and other notable Baies,and Capes of lande, and of the qualitie, and goodneſſe of thoſe groundes.

The next day being the ſeconde of Iuly we diſcouered and had ſight of land on the Noꝛtherne ſide towarde vs, that dyd ioyne vnto the lande aboueſayd, all compaſſed about, and we knewe that it had about * in dꝺpth, and as muche athwart, we named it Saint Lunarios Baie, ꝓ with our boates we went to the Cape toward the Noꝛth, and founde the land and grounde ſo lowe, that foꝛ the ſpace of a league from land there was but halfe a faddome water.On the Noꝛtheaſt ſide from the ſayde Cape about ſeauen oꝛ eight leagues there is another Cape of lande, in the middeſt whereof there is a Baie faſhioned triangle wiſe, verye dꝺpe, and as far as we could ken from it lieth Noꝛtheaſt.The ſaid Baie is compaſſed about w̃ ſands and ſhelues about ten leagues from land, and there is but one faddome water : from the ſaide Cape to the banke of the other,ther is about fiftꝺne leagues.We being acroſſe the ſayde Capes , diſcouered another lande and Cape,and as farre as we coulde ken,it lay Noꝛth ꝓ by Eaſt. All that night the weather was very ill, and great windes, ſo that we were conſtrained to beare a ſmall ſayle vntill the next moꝛning, being the thirde of Iuly,that the winde came from the Weſt : and we ſayled Noꝛthwarde, to haue a ſight of the lande that we had left on the Noꝛtheaſt ſide,aboue the lowe landes, among whiche high and lowe landes there is a Gulfe,oꝛ Bꝛeach, in ſome places about ſixe and twenty faddome dꝺpe, and fiftꝺne leagues in bꝛeadth, with varietie of landes, hoping to finde ſome paſſage thyther, we went euen as the paſſage of the Caſtels . The ſayde gulfe lyeth Eaſte Noꝛtheaſt,and Weſt Southweſt. The grounde that lyeth on the South ſide of the ſayde gulfe, is as gꝺd and eaſie to be

other Iron wares, and a red hat to giue vnto their Captain. Which when they saw, they also came on land, and broughte some of their skinnes, and so began to deale with vs, seeming to be very glad to haue our iron wares, and other things, stil dauncing with many other ceremonies, as with their handes to cast sea water on theyr heades. They gaue vs whatsoeuer they had, not keeping any thing, that they were constrained to go backe againe naked, and made vs signes that the nexte day they would come againe, and bring more skinnes wyth them.

¶ How that we hauing sent two of our men on lande with wares, there came about. 300.wilde mē with great gladnes. Of the quality of the Country, what it bringeth forth, and of the Baie called *The Baie of heate.*

Vpō Thursday being the eight of the moneth, bicause the winde was not good to go out with our ships, we set our boates in a readinesse to go to discouer the saide Baie, and ye daye we wente fifteene leagues within it. The nexte day, the winde and wether being faire, we sayled vntil noone, in which time we had notice of a great part of the sayd Baie, and how that vpon the lowe landes, there were other lands, with high mountaines : but seeing that there was no passage at al, wee began to turne backe again, taking our way along the coast, and sayling, we sawe certaine wilde men, that stode vpon the shore of a Lake, that is among the lowe groundes, who were making fires and smokes : we went thither, and founde that there was a Chanel of the sea, that did enter into the Lake, & setting our boates at one of the banckes of the Chanell, the wilde men with one of their boates came vnto vs, & brought vs peeces of Seales readie sodde, putting them vpon peeces of wood : then retyring themselues, they woulde make signes vnto vs, that they did giue them vs. We sente two men vnto them with Hatchets, kniues, beades, & other such like ware, whereat they were very glad, and by and by in clusters they

E.   came

came to the ſhoꝛe where we wer with their boates, bꝛinging with them ſkinnes, and other ſuch things as they had, to haue of our wares. They were moꝛe than thꝛée hundꝛed men, wo-men, and chilbꝛen: ſome of the women which came not ouer, we might ſée them ſtande vp to the knées in water, ſinging and dauncing, the other that had paſſed the riuer where we were, came verpe friendlye to vs, rubbing oure armes with their owne handes, then woulde they lifte them vppe to-warde heauen, ſhewing manye ſignes of gladneſſe : and in ſuch wiſe were we aſſured one of another, that we very fami-liarly beganne to trafficke of whatſoeuer they had, till they had nothing but their naked bodies, foꝛ they gaue vs al what soeuer they had, and that was but of ſmall value. We per-ceiued that this people might verie eaſily be conuerted to our religion. They go from place to place. They liue only with fiſhing. They haue an oꝛdinarie time to fiſh foꝛ their pꝛouiſi-on. The Countrey is hotter, than the Countrey of *Spaine*, and the faireſt that can poſſibly be found, altogither ſmooth, and leauel. There is no place, be it neuer so little, but it hathe ſome trées (yea albeit it be ſandie) oꝛ elſe is ful of wilde coꝛn, that hath an eare like vnto Rie: the coꝛn is like Oates, ſmall Peaſon as thicke as if they had bin ſown ⁊ plowed, white ⁊ red gooſeberies, ſtrawberies, blackberies, white ⁊ red Roſes, wt many other ficures, of very ſwéete and pleaſãt smel. Ther be alſo many goodly medowes ful of graſſe , ⁊ Lakes where gret plentie of Salmons be. They cal a Hatchet in their tõg Cochi, and a knife Bacon: we named it The Bay of Heate.

¶ Of another nation of wilde men: of their maners, liuing and clothing.

WE being certified that there was no paſſage thꝛough the ſaid Bay, we hoiſed ſaile, ⁊ went frõ S. Martines Creeke vpon Sonday being the twelfth of July, to go ⁊ diſcouer fur-ther in the ſaid Baie. and went along the ſea coaſt Eſtward about eightéene leagues, till we came to the Cape of *Prato*, where we found the tide very greate, but ſhallow, and the ſea ſtoꝛmie, ſtormie, ſo that we were conſtrained to draw toward ſhore, betwéene the ſaide Cape and an Ilande lying Eaſtwarde, about halfe a league from the Cape, where we caſt Ancker for that night. The next morning we hoiſed ſayle to trend ẙ ſaid coaſte about, which lyeth North Northeaſt . But there roſe ſuch a ſtormie and raging winde againſt vs, that we wer cõſtrained to come to the place againe, from whence we were come: There did we ſtay all that daye till the nexte, that wée hoiſed vp ſayle, and came to the middeſt of a riuer fiue or ſixe leagues from the Cape of *Prato* Northward, and being ouerthwart the ſaid riuer, there aroſe againe a contrarie winde, with great fogges and ſtormes. So that we were conſtrayned vpon Tuiſday, being the fourtéenth of the moneth, to enter into the riuer, and there did we ſtay til the ſixtéenth of the moneth, loking for faire weather to come out of it, on which day being Thurſdaye, the winde became ſo raging, that one of our ſhippes loſt an Ancker, and we were conſtrayned to go vp higher into the riuer ſeauen or eighte leagues, into a good harborough and ground, ẙ we with our boates found out, and through the euil weather, tempeſt, and darkeneſſe that was, we ſtayed in the ſaide harborough till the fiue and twentith of the month, that we coulde not come out: in the mean time we ſawe a greate multitude of wilde men that were fiſhing for Mackrels, whereof there is great ſtore. Their boats wer about fortie, and the perſons, what with men, women, and children, two hundred, which after they had haunted our cõpanie a while, they came very familiarly with their boates to ẙ ſides of our ſhips. We gaue thẽ kniues, combs, beades of glas, & other trifles of ſmal value, for which they made many ſignes of gladneſſe, lifting their handes vp to Heauen, dauncing and ſinging in their boates. Theſe men may very wel & truely be called Wilde, bicauſe there is no porer people in the world. For I thinke al that they had togither, beſides theyr boates and nets, was not worth fiue ſouce. They go altogither naked, ſauing their priuities, which couered with a little ſkinne, and certaine olde ſkinnes that they caſt vppon them.

Neyther

Neyther in nature nor in language, do they any whit agrée w̃
them we found first: Their heads be altogither shauen, except
one bush of haire, they suffer to grow vpon the toppe of theyr
crowne, as long as a horsse taile, and then with certaine lea-
ther strings binde it in a knot vpon their heades. They haue
no other dwelling but their boates, which they tourne vpside
down, and vnder them they lay themselues al along vpon the
bare ground. They eate their fleshe almosse rawe, onely that
they heate it a little vppon imbers of coles, so doe they theyr
fishe. Vpon Magdalens day we with our boates wente to the
bancke of the riuer, and frélye went on shore among them,
whereat they made many signes of gladnesse, and al their mẽ
in two or thrée companies began to sing and daunce, séeming
to be very glad of our comming. They had caused al the yõg
women to flée into the wood, two or thrée excepted, that stayed with them, to each of which we gaue a combe, and a little
bell made of Tinne, for which they were very glad, thanking
our Captaine, rubbing his armes and breastes with theyr
handes. When the men saw vs giue something vnto those
that had stayde, it caused all the rest to come out of the wood,
to the ende they should haue as muche as the others : These
women were about twentie, who altogither in a knot fell vpon our Captain, touching and rubbing him with their hãds,
accoding to their manner of cherishing and making muche
of one, who gaue to eache of them a little Tinne bell : then
sodainely they began to daunce, and sing many songs. There
we founde great store of Mackrels, that they had taken vpon
the shore, with certaine nettes that they make to fishe , of a
kinde of hempe that groweth in that place where ordinari-
lye they abide, for they neuer come to the sea, but onlye
in fishing time. As farre as I vnderstand, ther groweth likewise a kinde of Millet as bigge as small Peason, like vnto
that which groweth in *Bresil*, which they eat in stead of bread.
They had greate store of it. They call it in theyr tong R A-
P A I G E. They haue also Prunes, (that is to saye Damsins)
which they dry for winter as we do, they cal thẽ H O N E S T A.

They

They haue alſo Figges, Nuttes, Apples, and other fruites, and Beanes, that they cal S A H V, their Nuttes C A H E H Y A. If we ſhewed them any thing that they haue not, noꝛ knowe not what it is, ſhaking their heads, they will ſay N O H D A, whiche is as much to ſay, they haue it not, noꝛ they know it not. Of thoſe things they haue, they would with ſignes ſhew vs the way how to dꝛeſſe them, and how they grow. They eate nothing that hath any taſt of ſalte. They are very great Thæues, foꝛ they will filch and ſteale whatſoeuer they can lay hold of, and all is fiſh that commeth to net.

¶ How our men ſet vp a great Croſſe vpon the poynt of the ſayd Porte, and the Captayne of thoſe wild men, after a long Oration, was by our Captayne appeaſed, and contented that two of his Children ſhould goe with him.

Vpon the 24. of ỹ Moneth, we cauſed a faire high Croſſe to be made of the heigth of thirtie foote, which was made in the pꝛeſence of many of them, vpon the poynt of the entrance of the Gulfe, in the middeſt whereof, we hanged vp a Shæld with thꝛée Floure de Luces in it, and in the toppe was carued in the wood with Anticke letters this poſie, V i v E L E R O Y D E F R A N C E. Then befoꝛe them all we ſet it vp vpon the ſayd poynt. They with great héede beheld both the making and ſetting of it vp. So ſoone as it was vp, we altogither knéeled downe befoꝛe them, with our hands towarde Heauen, yéelding God thankes: and we made ſignes vnto them, ſhewing them the Heauens, and that all our ſaluation dependeth only on him which in them dwelleth: whereat they ſhewed a great admiration, looking firſt one at another, and then vpon the Croſſe. And after we were returned to oure Shippes, their Captayne clad with an old Beares Skinne, with thꝛée of his Sonnes, and a Bꝛother of his with him, came vnto vs in one of their Boates, but they came not ſo néere vs as they were wont to do: there he made a long Oꝛation vnto vs, ſhewing vs the croſſe we had ſet vp, and making

a Croſſe with two of his fingers, then did he ſhew vs all the
Countrey about vs, as if he would ſay that all was his, and
that we ſhould not ſet vp any Croſſe without his leaue. His
talke being ended, we ſhewed him an Are, ſayning that we
would giue it him for his ſkinne, to whiche he liſtned, for by
little and little he came néere our Ships. One of our fellowes
that was in our boate, tooke holde on theirs, & ſuddaynely lept
into it, with two or thrée more, who enforced him to enter into our Ships, whereat they were greatly aſtoniſhed. But our
Captaine did ſtraightwayes aſſure thẽ, that they ſhould haue
no harme, nor any iniury offered them at all, and entertained
them very frendly, making them eate and drinke. Then did
we ſhew them with ſignes, that the Croſſe was but only ſet
vp to be as a light and leader which wayes to enter into the
port, and that we would ſhortly come againe, and bring good
ſtore of iron wares and other things, but that we would take
two of his children with vs, and afterward bring them to the
ſaid port againe: and ſo we clothed two of them in ſhirtes, and
coloured coates, with red cappes, and put about euery ones
necke a copper chaine, whereat they were greatly contented:
then gaue they their old clothes to their fellowes that wente
backe againe, and we gaue to each one of thoſe thrée that wẽt
backe, a hatchet, and ſome kniues, which made thẽ very glad.
After theſe were gone, and had told the newes vnto their fellowes, in the after noone there came to our ſhips ſire boates
of them, with fiue or ſire men in euery one, to take their fare-
wels of thoſe two we had retained to take with vs, and
brought them ſome fiſh, vttering many words which we did
not vnderſtand, making ſignes that they woulde not remoue
the Croſſe we had ſet vp.

¶ How after we were departed from the ſaide porte, follo-
    wing our voiage along the ſayd coaſt, we went to diſco-
    uer the land lying South-eaſt, and North-weaſt.

The nexte daye, being the 25. of the moneth, we had faire
    weather, and went from the ſaid porte: and being out of
                                                            the

the Riuer, we ſailed Eaſt Nozth-eaſt, foz, after the entrance into the ſaid Riuer, the land is enuironed about, and maketh a bay in maner of halfe a circle, where being in our Ships, we might ſée al the coaſt ſayling behind, which we came to ſéeke, the land lying South-eaſt and Nozth-weaſt, the courſe of which was diſtant from the riuer about twentie leagues.

¶ Of the Cape *S. Aluiſe*, and *Momorancies Cape*, and certayne other lands, and how one of our Boates touched a
Rocke and ſuddainely went ouer it.

On monday being the 27. of the moneth, about ſunne ſet we went along the ſaide lande, as we haue ſayde, lying South-eaſt and Nozth-weaſt, til Wlenſday that we ſaw ano-
ther Cape, where the land beginneth to bend toward ẙ Eaſt: we went alongſt it about 15. leagues, then doth the land begin to turne Nozthward. About thzée leagues frô the ſayd Cape we ſounded, and found 12. faddome water. The ſaid lands are plaine, and the faireſt and moſt without woods that we haue ſéene, with goodly gréene féelds and medowes, we named the ſaid Cape S. Aluiſe Cape, bycauſe that was his day: it is 49. Degrées and a halfe in Latitude, and in Longitude. *. On Wlenſday mozning we were on the Eaſt ſide of the Cape, and being almoſt night, we went Nozth-eaſtward foz to appzoch nére to the ſaid land, which trédeth Nozth and South. From S. Aluiſe Cape, to another called Momorancies Cape, about fiftéene leagues, the lande beginneth to bende Nozth-
weaſt. About thzée leagues from the ſayd Cape, we woulde néedes ſounde, but we could finde no ground at 75. faddome, yet went we alongſt the ſayd land, about tenne leagues, to the Latitude of 50. degrées. The Saturday following, being the firſt of Auguſt, by Sunne riſing, we had ſight of certayne o-
ther landes, lying Nozth, and Nozth-eaſt, that were very high and craggie, and ſéemed to be mountaynes: betwéene which were other lowlands with Wloodes and Riuers: we wente aboute the ſayde landes, as well on the one ſide as

on

on the other, ſtill bending Noꝛth-weaſt, to ſẽe if it were either a Gulfe, oꝛ a paſſage, vntill the fifth of the moneth. The diſtance from one land to the other, is about fiftẽene leagues. The middle betwẽene them both, is 50. degrẽes and a thirde part of one in Latitude. We had much ado to go fiue miles farther, the winds were ſo great, and the tide againſt vs. And at fiue miles end, we might playnely ſẽe and perceyue land on both ſides, whiche there beginneth to ſpꝛeade it ſelfe, but bycauſe we rather-fell, than gote way againſt the winds, we went toward land, purpoſing to goe to another Cape of land, lying Southwarde, which was the fartherm oſt out into the Sea that we could ſẽe, about fiue leagues from vs, but ſo ſoone as we came thither, we founde it to be nought elſe but Rockes, ſtones, and craggie cliftes, ſuch as we had not found any where that we had ſayled Southwarde from S. Iohns Cape: and then was the tide with vs, which caryed vs againſt the winde Weſtwarde, ſo that as we were ſayling along the ſayd coaſt, one of our Boates touched a Rockẽ, and ſuddainely went ouer, but we were conſtrayned to leape out, foꝛ to direct it on accoꝛding to the tide.

¶ How after we had agreed and conſulted what was beſt to bee done, wee purpoſed to returne from *S.Peeters* ſtraight, and from *Tiennots* Cape.

After we had ſayled along the ſayd coaſt, foꝛ the ſpace of two houres, behold, the tyde began to turne againſte vs, with ſo ſwift and raging a courſe, that it was not poſsible foꝛ vs with thirtẽene oares to rowe oꝛ gette one ſtones caſt farther, that we were conſtrayned to leaue our Boates with ſome of our men to gard them, and tenne oꝛ twelue men went on ſhoare to the ſayd Cape, where we found that the land beginneth to bend South-weaſt, whiche hauing ſẽene, we came to our Boates againe, and ſo to oure Shippes, whiche were ſtill readie rigged, hoping to goe foꝛward : but foꝛ all that, they were fallen moꝛe than four leagues where we had lefte them,

them, where so soone as we came, we assembled togither all
our Captaynes, Maysters, and Marriners, to haue their ad-
uice and opinion what was best to be done : and after that e-
uery one had sayd, considering that the Easterly windes beganne to beare sway, and blow, and that the floud was so
great, that we did but fall, and that there was nothing to be
gotten, and that stormes and tempestes beganne to puffe in
those new Countreys, and that we were so farre from home,
not knowing the perils and dangers were behind, for eyther
we must agrée to turne and come backe againe, or else to stay
there all the yeare. Moreouer, we did consider, that if an ex-
chaunge of the Northerne windes did take vs, it were not possible for vs to depart thence. All which opinions being heard
and considered, we altogither determined to addresse oure
selues homeward. Now bycause vpon Saint Peeters day we
entred into the sayde straighte, we named it Saint Peeters
Straight. We sounded it in many places, in some we found
70. faddome water, in some 50. and néere the shoare but 30.
and cléere ground. From that day till Wensday following,
we had a good and prosperous gale of wind, that we trended
the sayd land about on the North East South-east, West
and North-weast sides: for such is the situation of it, excepted
one Cape of low lands that bendeth towarde South-east, a-
bout 25. leagues from the straight. In this place we sawe
certayne smokes, that the people of the Countrey made vppon the sayd Cape : but bycause the winde blew vs towarde
the coast, we went not to them, whiche when they saw, they
came with two Boates and twelue men vnto vs, and as
fréelie came vnto our Shippes, as if they had bin *French* men,
and gaue vs to vnderstande, that they came from the greate
Gulfe, and that Tiennot was their Captayne, who then
was vpon that Cape, making signes vnto vs, that they were
going home to their Countreys where we were come from
with our Shippes, and that they were laden with Fish. We
named the sayd Cape, Tiennots Cape. From the saide Cape
all the lande trendeth East South-east, and West Northweast.

F.

weſt. All the land lyeth low, very pleaſant, enuironed with ſand, where the ſea is entermingled with mariſhes and ſhallowes, the ſpace of twentie leagues : then doth the land begin to trend from Weaſt to Eaſt, North-eaſt altogither enuironed with Ilands two or three leagues from land, in whiche as farre as we could ſee , are many dangerous ſhealues more than foure or fiue leagues from land.

¶ How that vpon the ninth of Auguſt we entred within *White Sands*, and vpon the fifth of September we came to the port of *S. Malo.*

From the ſaid Wenſday, vntill Saturday following, we had a great wind from the South-weaſt, whiche cauſed vs to draw Eaſt North-eaſt, on which day we came to the Eaſterly partes of the new land, betweene the Barnes and the Doble Cape. There beganne great ſtormie winds comming from the Eaſt with great rage : wherefore we coaſted the Cape North North-weaſt, to ſearche the Northerne parte, which is (as we haue ſayd) all enuironed with Ilands , and being neere the ſaid Ilands and land, the wind turned into the South, which brought vs within the ſaid gulfe, ſo that the next day being the ninth of Auguſt, we by the grace of God entred within White Sands. And this is ſo much as we haue diſcouered. After that, vpon the fifteenth of Auguſt, being the feaſt of the Aſſumption of our Lady, after that we had heard ſeruice, we altogither departed from the porte of White Sands, and with a happie and proſperous weather, we came into the middle of the Sea, that is betweene the newe land and *Brittanie*, in which place we were toſt and turmoyled three dayes long with great ſtormes and windie tempeſts comming from the eaſt, which with the aide and aſſiſtance of God we ſuffered : then had we faire weather, and vpon the fifth of September, in the ſaid yeare, we came to the port of *S. Malo* whence we were come.

The

The language that is spoken in the Land newly discouered, called new Fraunce.

God	———	a Bow	———
the Sunne	Isnetz	Brasse	aignetaze
the Heauen	camet	the Brow	ansce
the Day		a Feather	yco
the Night	aiagla	the Moone	casmogan
Water	ame	the Earth	conda
Sand	estogatz	the Winde	canut
a Sayle	aganie	the Rayne	onnoscon
the Head	agonaze	Bread	cacacomy
the Throate	conguedo	the Sea	a met
the Nose	hehonguesto	a Shippe	casaomy
the Teeth	hesangue	a Man	vndo
the Nayles	agetascu	the Heares	hoc hosco
the Feete	ochedasco	the Eyes	vgata
the Legges	anoudasco	the Mouth	hache
a dead man	amocdaza	the Eares	hontasco
a Skinne	aionasea	the Armes	agescu
that Man	yca	a Woman	enrasesco
a Hatchet	asogne	a sicke Man	alouedeche
greene Fish	gadagoursere	Shoes	atta
good to be eaten	guesande	a Skin to couer a ⎰	ouscozon
Flesh	———	mãs priuy mēbers ⎱	vondico ⎰
Almonds	anougaza	red cloth	cahoneta
Figges	asconda	a Knife	agoheda
Gold	henyosco	a Macrell	agedoneta
the priuie members	assegnega	Nuttes	caheyra
an Arow	cacta	Apples	honesta
a greene Tree	haueda	Beanes	sahe
an earthen dish	audaco	a Swoord	achesco

Heere endeth the first relation of *Iames Carthiers* discouery of the new land called *New France*, translated into English out of Italian by   I. F.

Assai ben balla a chi fortuna suona.

F.ij.   A short

¶ A ſhorte and briefe narration of the Nauigation cauſed to be made by the King of France, to the Ilands of *Canada*, *Hochelaga*, *Saguenay*, and diuers others, which now are called *New France*, vvith a diſcourſe of the particulars, cuſtomes, and man- ners of the inhabitoures therein.

**

Chap. 1.

IN the yeare of our Lord 1535. vpon Whit- ſonday, being the 16. of *May*, by the comman- dement of our owne Captayne Iames Car- thier, and with a common accord, in the Ca- thedrall Churche of *S. Malo*, we deuoutely each one confeſſed our ſelues, and recepued the Sacrament: and all entring into the Quier of the ſayde Church, we preſented our ſelues befoe the Reuerend Father in Chiſt, the Lode Biſhop of *S. Malo*, who bleſſed vs all, be- ing in his Biſhops Roabes. The Wenſday following, bæ- ing the 19. of *May*, there roſe a good gale of winde, and there- foe we hoyſed Sayle with thæe Shippes, that is to ſay, the great Hermina, being in burthen about a hundeth, o a hun- deth and twentie Tunne, wherein the foeſayde Captayne Iames Carthier was Generall, and Maiſter Thomas Froſ- mont chiefe Mayſter, accompanyed with Mayſter Claudius of *Pont Briand*, Sonne to the Lod of *Monteceuell*, and Cupbea- rer to the Dolphin of *France*, Charles of *Pomeraias*, Iohn Pow- let, and other Gentlemen. In the ſecond Shippe called the little Hermina, being of thæſcoe Tunne burthen, were Captaynes vnder the ſaid Carthier, Mace Salobert, and May- ſter William Marie. In the third Shippe called the Heme- rillon, being of fotie Tunne in burthen, were Captaynes M. William Brittan, and M. Iames Maingare. So we ſayled with a good and poſperous wind, vntil the 20. of the ſaid mo- neth,

neth, at which time the weather tourned into stormes & tē-
pests, ȳ which with contrarie winds, and darkenesse, endured
so long ȳ our ships being without any rest, suffered as much
as any ships that euer went on seas: so that the 25. of June, by
reason of that foule and foggie weather, all our shippes loste
sight one of another, neyther sawe we one another againe tyll
we came to the newe lande where we had appointed to méet.
After we had lost one another, we in the Generals ship were
with contrarie windes tost to and fro on the sea, vntil the se-
uenth of July, vpon which daye we arriued and came to the
Iland called the Iland of Byrdes, which lyeth from the main
lande. 44. leagues. This Ilande is so full of byrdes, that all
our ships might easily haue bin fraighted with them, and yet
for the great number that there is, it wold not séeme that any
were taken away. We to victual our selues filled two boats
of them. This Iland hath the Pole eleuated. 49. degrées, and
40. minutes. Vpon the eight of the sayde moneth we sayled
further, and with a prosperous weather came to the Porte
called The Port of white Sandes, that is in the Baie called
The Baie of Castels, where we had purposed to méete and stay
togither the fiftéenth of the said month. In this place therfore
we loked for our felows, that is to say, the other two ships, til
the 26. of the moneth, on which daye both came togither. So
sone as our fellowes were come, we set our shippes in a readinesse, taking in both water, wood, and other necessaries. And
then on the 29. of the saide moneth, early in the morning wée
hoised saile to passe on further, and sailing alongst the Northerne coast that runneth Northeast and Southwest, til two
howres after Sunne set or there-aboutes, and then we cros-
sed along two Ilandes, whiche doe stretch further forth than
the others, whiche we called S. Williams Ilandes, being distant aboute 20. leagues or more from the Porte of *Brest*. All
the coast from the Castels to that place lyeth East & Weast,
Northeast and Southweast, hauing betwéene it sundrye little Ilandes, altogither barren and full of stones, wythoute
eyther earth or trées, excepted certayne Valleys onely. The

nexte

nexte daye being the laste of Iulye sauing one, we sayled on
(Westward to finde out other Ilands) which as yet we had
not founde, rij. leagues and a halfe, among whiche there is a
great Baye towarde the North all ful of Ilandes and great
créekes, where manye good harboroughes séeme to be : them
we named Saint Marthas Ilandes, from which about a league
and a halfe further into the sea, there is a dangerous shallow,
wherin are four or fiue rocks, which lye from Saint Marthas
Ilandes about vij. leagues as you passe into the said Ilands,
on the East and on ŷ West side , to which we came the said
day an houre after noone, and from that houre vntil midnight
we sailed about fiftéene leagues athwart a cape of ŷ lower
Ilands, which we named S. Germans Ilãds South-eastward
frõ whiche place about thrée leagues, there is a very dangerous shallow. Likewise betwéen S. Germans Cape & S. Marthas, about two leagues frõ the said Ilãds, there lyeth a bãck
of sand, vpon which banck ŷ water is but two fadome déepe,
& therfore séeing ŷ dãger of ŷ coast, we struck saile & went no
further ŷ night : The next day being ŷ last of July, we wente
al along the coast ŷ runneth East & west, West & by North,
which is al enuironed about wt Ilandes & drie sandes, and in
truth are very daungerous. The length frõ S. Germans Cape
to the said Ilands is about rviij. leagues & a half, at the ende
of which ther is a goodly plot of grounde full of huge & highe
trées, albeit the rest of the coast be compassed about wt sandes
wout any signe or shew of harboroughs, til we came to Thiennots Cape, which tendeth Northwest about vij. leagues
from ŷ forsaid Ilãds, which Thiennots Cape we noted in our
former voyage, & therfore we sailed on all that night West
Northwest, til it was day, & then the winde turned againste
vs, wherefore we wente to séeke a Hauen wherin we might
harbor our ships, & by good hap, found one fit for our purpose,
about vij. leagues & a half beyond Thiennots Cape, and that
we named S. Nicholas Hauen, it lyeth amidst foure Ilandes
that stretcheth into the sea. Vpon the next we for a token set
vp a woodden crosse. But note by the way that crosse must be
turned

turned Northeast, and then bending toward it, leaue it on the
left hand, and you shall finde thrée fadome water, and within
the Hauen but two. Also you are to take héede of two shelues
that leane outwarde halfe a league. All this coaste is full of
quicke sandes and very daungerous, albeit in sighte manye
good Hauens séeme to be there, yet is there nought else but
shelues and sandes. We staide and rested our selues in the
sayde Hauen, vntill the seauenth of August being Sundaye:
on whiche daye we hoysed sayle, and came towarde lande one
the neather side towarde Rabasts Cape, distant from the sayd
Hauen about twentie leagues North Northeast, and South
Southweast : but the nexte daye there rose a stormie and a
contrarie winde, and therefore we coulde finde no Hauen
there towarde the South. Thence we wente coasting along
toward the North, beyonde the aboue-sayde Hauen aboute
tenne leagues, where we founde a goodly greate gulfe, full of
Ilandes, passages, and entraunces towarde what winde soeuer you please to bend: for the knowledge of this gulfe there
is a greate Ilande that is a Cape of the maine lande, stretching somewhat further forth than the others, and aboute
two leagues wythin the lande, there is an Hill fashioned as
it were an heape of corne. We named the sayde Gulfe Saint
Laurence hys Baie. The twelfth of the sayde month we went
from the sayd S. Laurence hys Bay, or Gulfe, sayling West-
warde, and came to finde a Cape of maine lande on the
Northside of the Baye, that runneth from the saide Sainte
Laurence his Baie about fiue and twentie leagues West and
by South. And of the two wilde men whiche we toke in our
former voyage, it was tolde vs that this was of the Bande
towarde the South, and that there was an Ilande, on the
Southerlye parte of whiche is the waye to goe to *Honguedo*
where the yeare before we hadde taken them in *Canada*,
and that two dayes iourney from the sayde Cape, an I-
lande began the Kingdome of *Siguenay*, in the lande North-
warde extending towarde *Canada*, and aboute thrée leagues
athwart the saide Cape, there is aboue fiftie faddome déepe.

Moreouer

Moreouer I beléeue that there was neuer so many Whales séene as we sawe that day about the Cape. The next daye after our Ladie day in August, being the fiftéenth of the month, hauing past those straightes, where we had notice of certaine landes that we left toward the South, whiche landes are full of very high hilles, and therfore we named them The Ilands of the Assumption, and one Cape of the sayd high countryes lyeth East north-easte, and Weste south-west, the distaunce betwéene which, is about fiue & twentie leagues. The Countryes lying North, maye playnely be perceyued to be higher thã the Southerly more than thirtie leagues. We trended ý saide landes about towarde the South, frõ the said day vntyl Twesday noone following, the winde being in the West, and therfore we bended toward the North, purposing to go and sée the land that we before had spyed. Being arriued there, wée founde the sayd Ilands, as it were ioyned togither, and lowe toward the Sea. And the Northerly mountaines that are vpon the saide lowe Ilandes stretching Easte, Weste, and by Southe. Our men tolde vs that there was the beginning of *Saguenay*, and that it was land inhabited, and that thére commeth the redde Copper, of them named CAIGNETDAZE. There is betwéen the Southerly Ilands, and the Northerly about 30. leagues distance, and more thã 100. faddome depth. The saide men did moreouer certifye vnto vs, that there was the way and beginning of the gret riuer of *Hochelaga*, a ready way to *Canada*, which riuer the further it went the narower it came, euen vntil to *Canada*, and that then there was freshe water, which went so farre vpwards, that they hadde neuer hearde of any man had gone to the heade of it, and that there is no other passage but with small boates. Our Captayne hearing their talke, and how they did affirm no other passage to be there, woulde not at that time procéede any further, tyll he had séene and noted the other Ilandes, & coast towarde the North, which he had ommitted to sée, after Saint Larance his gulfe, bycause he would exquisitly know, if in the Ilandes toward the South any passage had bin discouered.

How

¶ How our Captain caused the shippes to retourne backe
again, only to know if in *Saint Laurence* gulfe there were
any passage towarde the North. CHAP. 2.

Vpon the 18. of August being Wednesday, our Captaine
caused his shippes to winde backe, and bend toward the
other shore, so that we trended the sayd Northerly cost, whiche runneth South-east, & North-west, being fashioned like
vnto halfe a bowe, and is a very high land, but yet not so high
as that on the Southerly partes. The Thursday following
we came to seuen very high Ilandes, whiche we named The
round Ilands. These Ilandes are distant from the others a-
bout fourtie leagues, and stretche out into the Sea aboute
thrée or foure leagues. Aboute these there are goodly lowe
groundes to be séene full of goodlye trées, whiche we the Fry-
day following, with our boates compassed aboute. Ouerthwart these Ilandes there are diuerse sandie shelues more
than two leagues into the sea, very daungerous, whiche at a
a lowe water remaine almost dry. At the furthest boundes of
these lowe Ilands, that containe about tenne leagues, ther is
a riuer of fresh water, that with such swiftnesse runneth into
the sea, that for the space of one league within it the water
is as freshe as anye fountaine water. We with our boates
entred into the saide riuer, at the entraunce of whiche we
found about one fadome water. There are in this riuer many
fishes shaped like horsses, which as our wilde men told vs, al
the daye long lye in the water, and the night on lande : of
which we sawe therein a great number. The next day being
the one and twentith of the month, by breake of day we hoysed sayle, and sayled so long about the sayde coaste, that wée
had sight of the Northerly partes of it, which as yet we had
not séene, and of the Iland of the Assumption whiche we had
founde, departing from the sayde land: which thing so soon as
we had done, and that we were certifyed no other passage to
be there, we came to our shippe againe, whiche we had left at

G. the

the said Ilands, where is a good harborough, the water being about nine or ten faddome. In the same place by occasion of contrarie winds and foggie mystes, we were constrayned to stay, not being either able to come out of it, or hoyse sayle til the four & twentith of the month. On which day we departed & came to a hauen on the Southerly coast, about 80. leagues from the said Ilands. This hauen is ouer against three flat Ilāds y lye amidst a riuer, bycause on the half way of y sayd Ilands, & the said Hauen toward the North, there is a verye great riuer that runneth betwéene the high & low Ilands, & more than thrée leagues into the sea: it hath many shelues, & there is not altogither one fadome water, so that the place is very dangerous: & from bank to bancke of the saide shelues, there is either xv. or xx. yardes. All the Northerly cost ráneth East Northeast and South Southwest. The saide hauen wherin we stayed, is as it were but a sluce of the waters that rise by the floud, and but of smal accompt, we named them S. Iohns Isleetes, bycause we founde them, and entred into thē the day of the beheading of that Saint. Aboute fiue leagues afore you come to the said hauen Westward, there is no passage at al but only with little boates. The hauen of S. Iohns Islettes, dryeth vp all the waters that rise by flowing, yea if it flowe a faddome. The best place to harborough ships therin is on the South part of a certaine little Islande that is ouer against the sayde hauen, whereby the bancke or shore of of the Iland riseth. Upon the first of September we departed out of the said hauen, purposing to go towarde *Canada*, and about 15. leagues from it towarde West Southwest, amidst y riuer there are thrée Ilandes, ouer against the whiche the riuer runneth swift, and is of a great depth, & it is that which leadeth, and runneth into the Countrey and kingdome of *Saguenay*, as by the two wilde men of *Canada* it was tolde vs. Thys riuer, passeth and runneth along very high and stéepe hilles of bare stone, where very little earth is, and notwithstanding there is greate quantitie of sundrie sortes of trées that growe in the sayde bare stones, euen as vppon good and

fertile

fertile grounde, in such sorte that we haue séene some so great
as well woulde suffise to make a maste for a shippe of fortie
Tunne burden, and as gréene as possible can be growing, in
a stonie rocke without any earth at all. At the entraunce of
the sayd riuer we mette with foure boates ful of wilde men,
whiche as farre as we coulde perceyue, verye fearefullye
came toward vs, so that some of them went backe agayne, &
the other came as neare vs as easilye they might heare and
vnderstond one of our wilde men, who tolde them his name,
and then toke acquaintaunce of them, vpon whose word they
came to vs. The nexte day, being the seconde of September,
we came out of the riuer to goe to *Canada*, and by reason of
the Seas flowing, the tide was verie swifte and daungerous
for that on the South part of it there lye two Ilandes, about
whiche more than thrée leagues compasse, lye manye greate
stones, and but two faddome water : and the flowing amidst
those Ilandes, is verye vnconstante and doubtefull, that if
it hadde not bene for our boates, we hadde bene in great dā-
ger to lose our liues : and coasting along the saide dry sands,
there is more than fiftéen faddome water. About fiue leagues
beyonde the riuer of *Saguenay* Southweast, there is another
Ilande more Northerly acrosse, whiche are certaine highe
péeces of lande , and thereaboutes we thought to haue caste
Ancker on purpose to staye the nexte tide, but we could sound
no ground by thrée score faddome within a slighte shote from
shoare, so that we were constrayned to winde backe to
the sayde Ilande , where wée sounded againe, and founde
eightéene faddome. The nexte mornyng we hoysed saile
and wente thence , sayling further on, where wée hadde
notice of a certayne kinde of fishe neuer to fore of a-
nye manne séene or knowen. They are aboute the bignesse of a Purpois, yet nothing like them, of bodye verye
well proportioned, headed lyke Graye-houndes, altogither as white as Snowe , wythout anye spotte, within
which Riuer there is great quantitie of them : they do liue
altogyther betwéene the Sea and the freshe Water.

G.ij. These

Those of the Countrey call them ADHOTHVYS, they tolde
vs that they be very sauozye and good to be eaten. Mozeouer
they affirme none to be found elſe-wher but in that riuer. The
firſt of the month, the weather being calme ¢ faire, we went
about fiftéene leagues moze vpward into the riuer, and there
lighted on an Iland that looketh Nozthward, and it maketh a
little hauen oz créeke wherin are many ¢ innumerable great
Toztoyzes, continuallye lying about that Ilande. There are
likewiſe great quantitie of the ſaid Aphothuys taken by the
inhabitours of the Coûtry, ſo that there is as gret concourſe
and méeting in that place as is at *Bordeous* in *Fraunce* at e-
uery tide. This Iland is in length about thzée leagues, and in
bzedth two , and is a goodly and fertile plot of ground, repleniſhed with many goodly and great trées of manye ſortes. A-
mong the reſt ther are many Filburde trées, which we found
hanging full of them, ſomewhat bigger and better in ſauour
than ours, but ſomewhat harder, and therefoze we called it
The Iland of Filburdes. The ſeuenth of the month, being our
Ladies euen, after ſeruice we went from that Ilande, to goe
vp higher into the riuer, and came to the Fourteene Ilandes,
ſeauen oz eight leagues from the Ilande of Filburdes, where
the Countrey of *Canada* beginneth, one of which Ilandes is
ten leagues in length, and fiue in bzedth, greatlye inhabited
of ſuch men as onlie liue by fiſhing of ſuche ſortes of fiſhes
as the riuer affourdeth, accozding to the ſeaſó of them. After
we had caſt Ancker betwéene the ſayde Ilande, and the Noz-
therly coaſt, we went on lande and tooke our two wilde men
with vs, méeting with many of thoſe Countrey people, who
woulde not at all appzoch vnto vs, but rather fledde from vs
vntill our two men beganne to ſpeake vnto them, telling thé
that they wer Taignoagny ¢ Domagaia, who ſo ſoone as they
had také aquaintance of thé, began greatly to reioyce, daun-
ſing and ſhewing many ſozts of ceremonies: and many of the
chiefeſt of thé came to our boats ¢ bzought many Eles, ¢ o-
ther ſozts of fiſhes, with two oz thzée burdens of great *Millet*
wherwith they make their bzead, ¢ many gret muſk milions.

The

The same daye came also manye other boates full of those
Countreymen and Women, to see and take aquaintance of
our two mé, al which were as courteously recepued, & friendly entertayned of our Captayne, as possible could be. And to
haue them the better acquaynted with him, and make them
his friends, he gaue them many small giftes, but of small value : neuerthelesse, they were greatly contented with them.
The next day following, the Lorde of *Canada* (whose proper
name was Donnacona) but by the name of Lorde, they call
him Agouhanna, with twelue boates came to our Ships,
accompanyed of many people, who causing tenne of hys
Boates to go backe with the other two, approched vnto vs
with sirtéene men more. Then began the sayde Agouhanna
being néerest vnto our Shippe, accordíng to their manner
and fashion, to frame a long Oration, mouing all his bodie
and members after a strange fashion, whiche thing is a Ce-
remonie and signe of gladnesse and securitie among them,
and then comming to the Generals Shippe, where Taignoagny, and Domagaia spake with them, and they with him,
where they began to tell and shewe vnto him what they had
séene in *Fraunce*, and what good entertainment they had had,
hearing which things, the Lorde séemed to be very glad of,
& prayed our Captain to reach him his arme, that he might
kisse it, whych thing he did: their Lord taking it, laid it about
his necke, for so they vse to do when they will make much of
one. Then our Captayne entred into Agouhannas boate,
causing bread and wine to be brought, to make the sayd Lord
and his companie to eate and drinke, which thing they did,
and were greatly thereby contented and satisfyed. Our Captayne for that time gaue them nothing, bycause he looked for
a fitter oportunitie. These things being done, each one toke
leaue of others, and the Lord went with his boates agayne
where he was come from. Our Captayne then caused oure
boates to be set in order, that with the next tide he might goe
vp higher into the Riuer, to finde some harborough wherein
to set our Ships : and the next tide we went coasting alongst

the said Iland, about tenne leagues, at the ende whereof, we found a goodly and pleasant sluce of water, where is another little riuer and hauen, where by reason of the flood there, is two faddome water. This place seemed to vs very fitte and commodious to put our ships therein, and so we did very safely, we named it the holy Crosse, for on that day we came thither. Neere vnto it, there is a village, whereof Donnacona is Lord, and there he keepeth his abode: it is called *Stadagona*, as goodly a plot of ground as possibly may be seene, and therewithall very fruitefull, full of goodly trees euen as in *France*, as Oakes, Elmes, Ashes, Walnut trees, Maple trees, Cidrons, Vines, and white Thornes, that bring forth fruite as big as any Damsons, and many other sortes of trees, vnder which groweth as faire tall hemp, as any in *France*, without any seede, or any mans worke or labour at all. Hauing considered the place, & finding it fit for our purpose, our Captayne withdrew himselfe on purpose to returne to our Shippes, but beholde, as we were comming out of the Riuer, we met comming against vs one of the Lords of that village *Stadagona*, accompanied with many others, as men, women, and childre, who after the fashion of their Countrey, in signe of mirth and ioy, began to make a long Oration, the Women still singing and dancing vp to the knees in water. Our Captayne knowing their good will and kindnesse towarde vs, caused the Boate wherein they were, to come vnto him, and gaue them certaine trifles, as kniues, and beades of glasse, whereat they were maruellous glad, for we being gone about 3. leagues fro them, for the pleasure they conceyued of our comming, we might heare the sing, & see the dance for all they were so farre.

¶ How our Captayne went to see and note the bignesse of the Iland, and the nature of it, and then returned to the Shippes, causing them to be brought to the Riuer of the holy Crosse. CHAP. 3.

After we were come with our Boates vnto our Shippes againe, our Captaine caused our Barkes to be made readie to

016d go on land in the sayde Ilande, to note the trées that
in shew séemed so faire, and to consider the nature and
qualitie of it, which thing we did, and found it full of good
lye trées like to ours. Also we sawe many goodly Uines, a
thing not tofore of vs séene in those Countreys, and therefore we named it Bacchus Iland. It is in length about twelue
leagues, in sight very pleasant, but full of woods, no parte of
it wrought, vnlesse it be in certaine places, where a few ho r-
ses be for Fishers dwellings, as before we haue sayde. The
next day we departed with our Ships to bring them to the
place of the holy Crosse, and on the 14. of that moneth we
came thither, and the Lorde Donnacona, Taignoagny, and
Domagaia, with 25. Boates full of those people, came to méete
vs, comming from the place whence we were come, and going toward Stadagona, where their abiding is, and all came
to our Ships, shewing sundrie and diuers gestures of gladnes and mirth, except those two that we had brought, to
witte, Taignoagny, & Domagaia, who séemed to haue altered
& changed their mind & purpose, for by no meanes they would
come vnto our Ships, albeit sundry times they were earnest-
ly desired to do it, wherbpon we began to mistrust somewhat.
Our Captayne asked the if according to promise they would
not go with him to Hochelaga, they answered yea, for so they
had purposed, and then each one withdrew himselfe. The next
day being the fiftenth of the moneth, our Captaine wente on
shore, to cause certaine poles and piles to be driuen into the
water, and set vp, that the better and safelyer we might set
our Shippe there: and to behold that, many of those Countrey
people came to méete vs there, among whome was Donnacona, and our two men, with the rest of their companye,
who kepte themselues aside vnder a poynt or nooke of lande
that is vppon the shoare of a certayne Riuer, and no one
of them came vnto vs as the other did that were not on their
syde. Our Captayne vnderstanding that they were there,
commaunded parte of oure menne to followe hym, and hee
went to the sayd poynt, where he found the sayd Donnacona,
                                        Taigno-

Taignoagny, Domagaia, & diuers other: and after salutations giuen on eache side, Taignoagny setled himselfe formost to speake to our Captayne, saying that ý Lord Donnacona did greatly grǽue and sorrow that our Captayne and his mē did weare warlike weapons, and they not. Our Captaine answered, that albeit it did grǽue them, yet would not he leaue thé of, and that (as he knew) it was ý maner of *France*. But for all these words, our Captayne and Donnacona left not off to speake one to another, and frǽndly to entertaine one another. Then did we perceyue, that whatsoeuer Taignoagny spake, was only long of himself, and of his fellow, for that our Captaine departed thence. He and Donnacona entred into a maruellous stedfast league of friendship, whereby all his people at once with a loude voyce, cast out thrée great cryes, (a horrible thing to heare) and each one hauing taken licence of the other for that day, we wente a word agayne. The day following, we put our two great Shippes within the Riuer and harborough, where the waters being at the highest, are but one fadome and halfe dǽpe, and at the lowest, but halfe a fadome. We left our Galion without the sluce, to the ende we might bring it to *Hochelaga*. So sone as we had safely placed our Shippes, behold, we saw Donnacona, Taignoagny, and Domagaia, with more than fiue hundred persons, men, women, and children, and the Lorde with tenne or twelue of the chiefest of the Countrey came a word of our shippes, who were all courteously receyued, and friendly entertayned, both of our Captayne, and of all vs: and diuers giftes of small value were giuen them. Then did Taignoagny tell our Captayne, that his Lord did greatly sorrow that he woulde go to *Hochelaga*, and that he would not by any meanes permit that any of them should goe with him, and that the Riuer was of no importance. Our Captayne answered him, that for all his saying, he woulde not leaue off his going thither, if by anye meanes it were possible, for that he was commanded by his King to goe as farre as possibly he could : and that if he (that is to say Taignoagny) would go with him, as he had promi-

sed,

fed he fhoulde be very wel entertained, befide that, he fhould
haue fuch a gifte giuen him, as he fhou lde wel content him-
felfe : fo2 hée fhoulde doe nothing elfe but goe with hym to
Hochelaga, and come againe . To whome Taignoagny aun-
fwered, that he woulde not by any meanes go, and thereup-
on fodainely returned to their houfes . The nexte day beyng
the 17.of September, Donnacona retourned euen as at the
firfte, and b2ought with him many Eeles, with fund2y fo2ts
of other fifhes, whereof they take greate fto2e in the fayde
Riuer, as mo2e largely hereafter fhall be fhewed . And as
foone as they were come to our Shippes, acco2ding to their
wonted vfe beganne to fing and daunce. This done, Donnacona caufed all his people to be fette of one fide, then making
a rounde circle vpon the Sand, caufed our Captaine with al
his people to enter therein, then he beganne to make a long
O2ation: holding in one of his handes a Maiden child 10.o2
12.yeares olde, whych he p2efented vnto our Captaine:then
fodainely beganne his people to fende out th2ée fh2ækes o2
howles, in figne of ioy and league of friendfhippe, p2efently
vpon that he did p2efent vnto him two other yong Male chil-
d2en one after another, but yonger than the other, at the gy-
uing of whyche, euen as befo2e, they gaue oute fh2ækes and
howles very lowde, with other ceremonies: fo2 whyche p2e-
fents, our Captaine gaue the faide Lo2de greate and hearty
thankes. The Lo2d tolde our Captaine then, that one of the
child2en was his owne b2other, and that the Maiden childe
was daughter vnto his owne fifter, and thefe p2efents were
onely giuen him, to the end he fhould not goe to Hochelaga at
all, to whome our Captaine anfwered, that if they were
onely giuen hym to that intent, if fo he would he fhould take
them againe, fo2 that by no meanes he woulde leaue hys
goyng off,fo2 as much as he was commaunded of his King.
But concerning this, Domagaia tolde oure Captaine, that
their Lo2de had gyuen him thofe child2en as a figne and token of goodwill and friendfhippe, and that he was contented
to goe wyth him to Hochelaga, vppon whyche talke greate

wordes arose betwene Taignoagny and Domagaia, by whyche we plainely perceyued that Taignoagny was but a craf-
tie knaue, and that he pretended but mischiefe and treason,
as well by thys dæde as others that we by hym hadde
séene. After that our Captaine caused the saide chyldren to
be putte in oure shippes, and caused two Swordes, and two
copper Wasens, the one wrought, the other plaine, to be broughte vnto hym, and them he gaue to Donnacona, who was
therewyth greately contented, yelding most hartye thankes
vnto our Captain for them, and presently vpon that he commaunded all his people to sing and daunce, and desired oure
Captaine to cause a péece of artillerie to be shot off, bycause
Taignoagny and Domagaia made great brags of it, and had
tolde them maruellous things, and also, bycause they had neuer hearde nor séene any before: to whome our Captaine answered, most willingly: and by and by commaunded his men
to shoote off 12. cannons charged with bullettes, acrosse the
wud that was hard by those people and ships, at whose noise
they were greatly astonished and amazed, for they thoughte
that Heauen had fallen vppon them, and put themselues to
flight, howling, crying, and shrieking, that it sæmed hel were
broken lose. But before we went thence, Taignoagny caused other men to tell vs, that those men whyche we had lefte
in our Gallion at roade, had slaine two men of theyr company, wyth a péece that they had shotte off, wherevppon the
reste had put themselues all to flight, as thoughe they should
all haue bene slaine, whych afterward we found vntrue, bicause our men had not shotte off any péece at all that daye.

¶ Howe *Donnacona*, *Taignoagny*, with others, deuised a pret-
tie slight or pollicie: for they caused three of theyr men
to be attyred like Diuels, fayning to be sent from theyr
God *Cudruaigny*, onely to hinder our voyage to *Hoche-*
laga. CHAP. 4.

The nexte day being the eightéenth of September, these
men still endeauoured themselues to séeke all meanes
possi-

possible to hinder and let our going to *Hochelaga*, and deuised
a pretty guile, as hereafter shall be shewed. They went and
dressed three men like Diuels, beyng wrapped in dogs skins
white and blacke, theyr faces besmeared as blacke as anye
coales, wyth hornes on theyr heads moze than a yard long,
and caused them secreatly to be putte in one of theyr boates,
but came not neere our shippes as they were wont to do, for
they lay hidden wythin the wood for the space of two houres,
loking for the tyde, to the end, the boate wherin the Diuels
were, might apprroch and come neare vs, whych, when time
was, came, and all the reste issued out of the wood commyng
to vs, but yet not so neare as they were wonted to do. There
began Taignoagny to salute oure Captaine, who asked hym
if he woulde haue the boate to come for hym, he aunswered,
not for that time, but after a while he woulde come vnto our
shippes: then presently came that boate rushing out, wherein
the three diuels were with such long hornes on theyr heades,
and the middlemost came making a long Oration, & passed a
long our shippes without turning or loking toward vs, but
with the boate wente to strike on lande. Then dydde Donnacona wyth all his people pursue them, and lay holde on the
boate and Diuels, who so soone as the menne were come to
them, fell prostrate in the boate euen as if they hadde beene
dead: then were they taken vppe and carried into the Wood,
beeyng but a stones cast off, then euery one wythdrewe himselfe into the wood, not onely staying behinde with vs, where
beyng, they beganne to make a long discourse, so lowde, that
we myghte heare them in oure shippes, whiche lasted aboue
halfe an houre, and beyng ended, we gan to espie Taignoagny and Domagaia comming towards vs, holding their handes ioyned togyther, carying their hattes vnder theyr
vpper garment, shewyng a greate admiration, and Taignoagny lokyng vppe to Heauen, cryed three tymes Iesus,
Iesus, Iesus, and Domagaia dwyng as hys fellow had done
before, cryed, Iesus Maria. Iames Carthier oure Capitaine
hearing them, and seeyng their gestures & ceremonies, asked

of them what they ayled, and what was happened or chaun-
ced anew, they aunswered, that there were very ill tydyngs
befallen, saying in French, *Nenni est il bon*, that is to saye, it
was not good: our Captaine asked them again, what it was,
then answered they, that theyr Lord Cudruaigny had spoken in *Hochelaga*, and that he had sent those thrée men to shew
vnto them that there was so muche Ice and Snowe by the
way, that whosoeuer went thither shoulde dye, whych wordes when we heard, we laughed, and mocked them, saying,
that their God Cudruaigny was but a foole and a noddy, for
he knewe not what he did or saide: then bade we them shewe
his messengers from vs, that Chrift woulde defende them al
from colde, if they woulde goe with him. Then did they aske
of our Captaine, if he had spoken with him, he aunsweared,
no, but that his ministers had, and that he had tolde them
they shoulde haue fayre weather: whiche words when they
had heard, they thanked our Captaine, and departed toward
the woodde to tell those newes vnto their fellowes, who sodainely came all rushing out of the woodde, séeming to be very glad for those wordes that our Captaine had spoken, and
to shew, that therby they had had, and felt great ioy. So sone
as they were before our Shippes, they altogither gaue oute
thrée great shréekes, and therevpon began to sing and dance,
as they were wont to doe. But for a resolution of the matter
Taignoagny and Domagaia tolde our Captaine, that theyr
Lorde Donnacona woulde by no meanes permitte that any
of them shoulde goe with him to *Hochelaga*, vnlesse he would
leaue hym some hostage to stay with him, our Captaine answered them, that if they would not go with him with a good
will, they should stay, for he would not by any meanes leaue
his going off, but woulde by all meanes possible endeauour
himselfe to goe thither if he coulde.

How

¶ Howe oure Captayne, wyth all his Gentlemenne, and fiftie Marriners, departed wyth oure Gallion, and the two boates of *Canada* to go to *Hochelaga*, and also there is described, what by the way and vppon the riuer was seene. CHAP. 5.

The next day being the 19. of September we hoised saile, and with our Gallion and two boates departed to go vp the riuer with the floude, where on both shoares of it we beganne to sée as goodly a countrey as possibly can with eye be séene, all replenished with very goodly trées, and Uines laden as full of Grapes as coulde be all along the riuer; whyche rather séemed to haue bene planted and wrought by handy worke than otherwise. True it is, that bycause they are not dressed and wrought as they shoulde be, theyr bunches of Grapes are not so great as ours, also we sawe all along the riuer many houses inhabited of Fishers, whyche take all kyndes of fishes, and they with great familiaritie and kindnesse came vnto vs, euen as if we had bene theyr Countreymen, and brought vs greate store of fishe, suche as they hadde with other thyngs, whyche we exchaunged with them for other wares, who lifting vp their hands toward heauen, gaue many signes of ioy: we stayed at a place called *Hochelas*, about 25. leagues from *Canada*, where the riuer wareth very narrowe, and runneth very swift, wherefore it is very dangerous, not only for that, but also for certain gret stones that are therein: Many boates and barkes came vnto vs, in one of whyche came one of the chiefe Lordes of the Countrey, making a long discourse, who beyng come néere vs, did by euident signes and gestures shewe vs, that the higher the Riuer went, the more daungerous it was, and bade vs take héede of our selues. The saide Lorde presented and gaue vnto our Captaine two of his owne childzen, of whyche oure Captaine toke one being a wench seuen or eight yeres old, the man child he gaue him againe, bycause it was to yong,

H.iij.   for

for it was but three yeares olde. Our Captaine as friendly
and as courteously dyd entertaine and receyue the sayd Lord
and his company, giuing thē certaine small trifles, & so they
departed towarde shoare againe. Afterwards the said Lord,
his wife, and his daughter, came to visite oure Capitayne at
Canada, bringing hym certaine small presents. From the 19.
vntill the 28. of September, wée sailed vp along the saide riuer, neuer losing one houre of time, all whyche time we saw
as godly and pleasant a Country as possibly can be wished
for, full (as we haue saide before) of all sortes of godlye
trées, that is to say, Oakes, Elmes, Walnut-trées, Ce-
drons, Firres, Ashes, Bore, Willowes, and greate store
of Vines, all as full of Grapes as coulde be, that if anye of
our fellowes went on shoare, they came home laden wyth
them : there are likewise many Cranes, Swannes, Géese,
Duckes, Feasants, Partridges, Thrushes, Blacke-birdes,
Turtles, Finches, Redbreastes, Nightingales, Sparrowes,
with many other sorts of Birds, euen as in *France*, and great
plentie and store. Vpon the 28. of September, wée came to
a gret wide lake in the middle of ỹ riuer fiue or sire leagues
broade, and twelue long, all that day we wente againste the
tide, hauyng but one faddome water, still kéeping the saide
scantling: beyng come to one of the heades of the Lake, wée
coulde espye no passage or going out, nay, rather it séemed
to haue bene closed and shutte vppe rounde about, and there
was but halfe a faddome water, lyttle more or lesse. And
therefore we were constrayned to casse Ancker, and staye
with our Gallion, and wente with oure two boates to séeke
some going out, and in one place we found four or fiue branches, whyche out of the riuer come into the Lake, and they
come from *Hochelaga*. But in the saide braunches, bicause of
the greate fiercenesse and swiftnesse wherewith they breake
out, and the course of the water, they make certaine Créekes,
and goings acrosse, yet at that time there was but halfe a
faddome water. Those Créekes beyng passed, we found
thrée faddome, and as farre as we could perceiue by the floud

                                            it

It was that time of the yeare that the waters are lowest, for at other times they flowe higher by two faddomes. All these foure or fiue branches do compasse about fiue or sixe Ilandes very pleasaunt, and thereby riseth the end of the Lake, about 15.leagues beyond, they all do come into one. That day wée landed in one of the saide Ilands, and met with fiue men that were hunting of wild beasts, who fréely and familiarly came to our boates without anye feare, as if we hadde euer béene brought vp togither. Our boates beyng somewhat neare the shoare, one of them tooke our Captaine in his armes, and caried him on shoare, as lightly and as easilie, as if he had bene a child of fiue olde: so strong and sturdy are those people. We founde, that they had a greate heape of wilde Mice that lyue in the water, as big as a Conny, and very good to eate, which they gaue vnto our Captaine, who for a recompence gaue them kniues and glazen Beades. Wée asked thē with signes if that was the way to *Hochelaga*, they aunswered yea, and that we had yet thrée dayes sayling thither.

¶ Howe our Captaine caused our Boates to be mended and dressed to goe to *Hochelaga* : and bycause the way was somewhat difficult and harde, we left our Gallion behinde: and howe we came thither, and what entertainement wee had of the people.　CHAP. 6.

The nexte day our Captaine séeyng, that for that tyme it was not possible for our Gallion to goe on anye further, hée caused oure Boates to bée made readye, and as muche munition and victualles to bée putte in them, as they coulde well beare : hæ departed wyth them, accompanyed wyth manye Gentlemen, that is to saye, Claudius of *Ponte Briand*, Cup-bearer to the Lorde Dolphin of *Fraunce* : Charles of *Poueray*: Iohn Gouion : Iohn Powlet: with twēty and eight marriners; and Mace Iallobert, and
William

William the Britton, who had the charge vnder the Captain of the other two shippes, to go vp as farre as they could into that riuer: wesailed with good and prosperous weather vntill the ninetéenth of October, on whiche daye we came to the towne of *Hochelaga*, distant from the place where we had left our Gallion 45. leagues. In whych place of *Hochelaga*, and all the waye we went, we met with many of those countrimen, who brought vs fishe, and suche other victualles as they had, still dauncing, and greatly reioycing at oure comming. Our Captaine, to lure them in, and to kéepe them our friends, to recompence them, gaue them kniues, beades, and such small trifles, wherewith they were greatly satisfied. So soone as we were come néere *Hochelaga*, there came to méete vs aboue a thousand persons, men, women and childzen, who afterwarde did friendly and merely entertaine and receyue vs as anye father woulde do his childe, whiche he had not of long tyme séene, the men dauncing on one side, the women on an other, and likewise the childzen on an other: after that they brought vs great stoze of fish, & of their breade made of Millet, casting them into oure Shippes so thicke, that you would haue thoughte it to fall from heauen. Whiche when our Captaine sawe, he, wyth many of hys companye wente on shoare: so soone as euer we were alande, they came clustring aboute vs, making very muche of vs, bzynging theyz yong childzen in theyz armes, onely to haue oure Capitaine & his company to touch them, making signes and shewes of great myzth & gladnes, that lasted moze than halfe an houre. Our Captaine séeyng theyz louing kindnesse and entertainment of vs, caused all the women ozderly to be set in a raye, and gaue them Beades made of Tin, and other suche small trifles, and to some of the men he gaue kniues: then he returned to the boates to supper, and so passed that night, all whiche while all those people abode on the shoare as neare oure boates as they might, making great fiers, and dauncing very merily, still crying, *Aguiaze*, which in their tongue signifieth Myrth and Safetie.

How

¶ How our Captayne with fiue Gentlemen, and twentie
armed men, all well in order, went to see the Towne of
Hochelaga, and the scituation of it.   CHAP. 7.

Our Captayne the next day very early in the morning,
hauing very gorgeously attired himselfe, caused all his
company to be set in order to go to see the Towne and habitation of those people, and a certaine Mountayne that is somewhat neere the Citie : with whome went also fiue Gentlemen, and twentie Marriners, leauing the rest to keepe and
loke to our Boates : we toke with vs three men of *Hochela-*
ga to bring vs to the place. All along as we went, we founde
the way as well beaten and frequented as can be, the fayrest
and best Countrey that possibly can be seene, full of as goodly
great Oakes as are in any wood in *France,* vnder whiche the
ground was all couered ouer with faire Akornes. After we
had gone about foure or fiue leagues, we met by the way one
of the chiefest Lords of the Citie, accompanyed with manye
mo, who so soone as he saw vs, beckned and made signes vnto vs, that we must rest vs in that place, where they had made
a great fire, and so we did. After that we had rested oure
selues there a while, the sayd Lord began to make a long discourse, euen as we haue sayd aboue they are accustomed to
do in signe of mirth and frendship, shewing our Captayne
and all his company a ioyfull countenance, and good will,
who gaue him two hatchets, a paire of kniues, and a Crosse,
whiche he made him to kisse, and then put it about his necke,
for whiche he gaue our Captayne heartie thankes.   This
done, we wente along, and about a league and a halfe farther, we beganne to find goodly and large feeldes, full of suche
Corne as the Countrey yeeldeth. It is euen as the Millet of
Bresill, as great, and somewhat bigger than small Peason,
wherewith they liue euen as we do with ours. In the midst
of those feeldes is the Citie of *Hochelaga,* placed neere, and as
it were ioyned to a great Mountaine, that is tilled round a-
I.   bout,

boute, very fertile, on the toppe of whiche, you may see verye farre, wée named it Mounte Roiall. The Cittie of
Hochelaga is rounde, compassed aboute with timber, with
thrée course of Rampires, one within another, framed
like a sharpe Spire, but layde acrosse aboue. The middlemost of them is made and builte as a directe line, but per-
pendicular. The Rampires are framed and fashioned with
péces of Timber, layde along on the grounde, very well
and cunningly ioyned togither after their fashion. This en-
closure is in heigth aboute two roddes. It hathe but one
Gate or entrie thereat, whiche is shutte with piles, stakes,
and barres. Ouer it, and also in many places of the wall,
there be places to runne along, and Ladders to gette vp,
all full of stones, for the defence of it. There are in the
Towne aboute fiftie houses, aboute fiftie paces long, and
twelue, or fiftéene broade, builte all of woode, couered o-
uer with the barke of the woode, as broade as any borde,
very finely and cunningly ioyned togither. Within the
sayde Houses, there are manye roomthes, Lodgings, and
Chambers. In the middest of euery one there is a greate
Courte, in the middle whereof they make their fire. They
liue in commons togither: then do the Husbandes, Wiues,
and Childern, eache one retire themselues to their Chambers. They haue also on the toppe of their Houses certayne Garets, wherein they képe their Corne to make
their bread withall: they call it CARRACONNY, which
they make as héereafter shall followe. They haue certayne péces of woode, made hollowe, like those where-
on wée beate oure Hempe, and with certayne Béetles
of woode they beate their Corne to powder: then they
make paste of it, and of the paste, Cakes, or else Tartes,
then lay them on a broade and hote stone, and then couer
it with hote Tiles, and so they bake their Bread, in stead
of Ouens. They make also sundrye sortes of Pottage
with the sayde Corne of Pease, and of Beanes, whereof they haue greate store: also with other fruites, as
                                                        Muſh

Puske Pillïgns, very greate Cowcombers. They haue also in their Houses certayne Uessels, as bigge as anye
Boate, o2 Tunne, wherein they p2eserue and kéepe their
fishe, causing the same in Sommer to be d2yed in the Sunne,
and liue therewith in Winter, whereof they make greate
p2ouision, as we by experience haue séene. All their viandes
and meates are without any tast o2 sauoure of salt at all.
They sléepe vpon barkes of Trées layde all along vpon the
grounde, with the Skinnes of certayne wilde Beastes,
wherewith they also cloth and couer themselues. The thing
most p2etious that they haue in all the Wo2lde, they call it
ESVRGNY: it is as white as any Snowe: they take it in
the Riuer of *Cornibotz*, in the manner as héere followeth.
When any one hath deserued death, o2 that they take any
of their enimies in Warres, first they kill him, then wyth
certayne great kniues they giue great slashes and strokes vppon the buttockes, flanckes, thighes, and shoulders: then
they cast the same body so mangled, downe to the bottome
of the Riuer, in a place where it is, called *Esurgny*, and there
leaue it tenne o2 twelue houres, then they take it vp againe,
and in the cuttes finde those. Of them they make beades,
and weare them aboute their neckes, euen as we do them of
golde, accompting it the p2etiousest thing in the Wo2lde.
They haue this vertue and p2opertie in them, they wyll
stoppe o2 stench any bléeding at the nose, fo2 we haue p2oued
it. These people are giuen to no other exercise, but onely to
husband2ie, and fishing wherewith to liue, they haue no care
of any other wealth o2 commoditie in this wo2ld, fo2 they
haue no knowledge of it, and that is, bycause they neuer
trauell and goe out of they2 Countrey, as those of *Canada*,
and *Siguenay* do, albeit the *Canadians* with eyghte o2 nine
Uillages mo2e alongst that Riuer bée subiectes vnto
them.

I ij.   ¶ How

¶ How we came to the Towne of *Hochelaga* , and the
entertaynemente there we had , and of certayne giftes
oure Captayne gaue them , with diuers other things.
CHAP. 8.

SO ſone as we were come néere the Towne, a greate
number of the inhabitoures thereof came to preſente
themſelues befoze vs after their faſhion, making very much
of vs : we were by our guides bzought into the midſt of the
Towne. They haue in the middlemoſt parte of their houſes
a large ſquare place, béeing from ſide to ſide a good ſtones
caſt, where we were bzought , and there with ſignes were
commaunded to ſtay : then ſuddaynely all the Women and
Maydens of the Towne gathered themſelues togither, parte
of which had their armes full of yong Childzen, and as ma-
nie as could, came to rubbe our faces, our armes, and what
parte of the bodye ſoeuer they could touch, wéeping foz verye
ioy that they ſaw vs, ſhewing vs the beſt countenance that
poſſible was, deſiring vs with theyz ſignes, that it woulde
pleaſe vs to touche theyz Childzen.   That done, the menne
cauſed the Women to withdzawe themſelues backe, then
they euery one ſate downe on the ground round about vs, as
if they would haue ſhewen and rehearſed ſome Comedie, oz
other ſhew : then pzeſently came the Women agayne, euery
one bzinging a foureſquare Matte in manner of Carpettes,
and ſpzeading them abzoad on the ground in that place : then
they cauſed vs to ſit vpon them. That done, the Lozd ⁊ King
of ỹ country was bzought vpon nine oz ten mens ſhoulders,
(whoſme in theyz toung they call A GOVHANNA) ſitting
vpon a great Stagges Skinne, and they layde him downe
vpon the forſayde mattes néere to our Captayne, euery one
beckning vnto vs that he was theyz Lozd and King. This
Agouhanna was a manne aboute fiftie yeares olde : he was
no whitte better apparelled than any of the reſt, onely excepted,

cepted,that he had a certaine thing made of beaſts Skinnes
(called *Ricci*) like a redde towell, and that was in ſteade of
his Crowne. He was full of the palſey , and his members
ſhronke togither . After he had with certayne ſignes and
beckes ſaluted our Captaine and all his company , and by
manifeſt tokens bidde vs all welcome , he ſhewed his
legges and armes to our Captaine, and with ſignes deſired him to touch them, and ſo he did, rubbing them with hys
owne hands : then did Agouhanna take the wreath or crown
he had about his head, and gaue it vnto our Captaine, that
done, they broughte before him diuerſe diſeaſed men , ſome
blinde, ſome criple, ſome lame and impotent , and ſome ſo
olde that the heare of their eyeleeds came downe and couered
their Cheekes, and laide them al along before our Captaine,
to the ende they mighte of him be touched : for it ſeemed vnto
them that God hadde bene deſcended and come downe from
Heauen to heale them. Our Captaine ſeeing the miſery and
deuotió of this poore people, recited the Goſpel of Saint Iohn,
that is to ſaye, In the beginning was the word : touching euerie one that were diſeaſed, praying to God that it wold pleaſe
him to open the harts of this poore people, and to make them
knowe his holy worde, and that they might receiue baptiſme
and Chriſtendome : that done, he toke a booke in his hande, &
with a lowde voyce redde all the paſſion of Chriſt, worde by
word, that al the byſtanders might hear him, al which while
this poore people kept ſilence, & were maruellouſly attentiue,
loking vp to heauē,& imitating vs in geſturs. Thē he cauſed
he'men al orderly to be ſet on one ſide, ẙ womē on another, &
likewiſe the childrē on another, and to the chiefeſt of them
he gaue Hatchets, to the other kniues , and to the women
beades, and ſuch other ſmal trifles. Then where the childrē
were, he caſte rings, counters, and branches made of Tin,
whereat they ſeemed to be verie gladde. That done, our Captaine commaunded Shawmes, and other muſical inſtrumēts
to be ſounded, which when they heard, they were very merrie. Then we toke our leaue and wente to our boate : the wo-

mē seeing that, put themselues before to stay vs, and brought
vs out of their meates that they had made readie for vs, as
fishe, pottage, beanes, and suche other things, thinking to
make vs eate, and dine in that place : but bycause the meats
hadde no sauoure at all of salte, we liked them not, but thanked them, and with signes gaue them to vnderstand that we
hadde no néede to eate. When we were out of the Towne,
diuerse of the men and women followed vs, and broughte
vs to the toppe of the forsayde mountaine, which we named
Mount Roiall, it is aboute a league from the Town. When
as we were on the top of it, we myght discerne, and plainely sée thirtie leagues off. On the Northe side of it there
are manye hilles to be séene, running Weasse and Easte,
and as manye more on the South, amongst and betwéene
the whiche the Countrey is as fayre and as pleasaunte as
possiblye can bée séene, being leauell, smoothe, and verye
playne, fitte to be husbanded and tilled : and in the middest
of those fieldes wée mighte sée further a greate waye
than where wée hadde lefte oure boates, where was the
greatest and the swiftest fall of water that anye where
hathe béen séene, as greate, wide, and large, as oure
sighte myghte discerne, goyng Southweast along thrée
fayre and rounde Mountaines that we sawe, as we iud-
ged aboute fiftéene leagues from vs. Those whiche broughte vs thyther, tolde and shewed vs, that in the sayde
Ryuer there were thrée suche falles of water more,
as that was where we hadde lefte oure boates : but bicause we coulde not vnderstande theyr language, we
coulde not knowe howe farre they were one from another. Moreouer, they shewed vs wyth signes, that the sayde
thrée falles being paste, a manne myghte sayle the space
of thrée moneths more alongst that Riuer, and that a-
long the Hilles that are on the Northe side, there is a
greate Riuer, whyche euen as the other commeth from
the Easte, wée thoughte it to bée the Riuer that runneth
through

throughe the Countrey of *Saguenay*: and wythoute anye
signe or question moued or asked of them, they toke the
chayne of oure Captaines whistell, whiche was of siluer,
and the dagger hafte of one of oure fellowe Marriners,
hangyng on hys side, being of yellowe Copper, guilte,
and shewed vs that suche stuffe came from the sayde Riuer, and that there bée *Agouionda*, that is as muche to
saye, as euill people, who goe all armed euen to their
fingers endes. Also they shewed vs the manner and making of theyr armoure: they are made of coardes and
woodde, finelye and cunninglye wroughte togyther. They
gaue vs also to vnderstande that those *Agouionda*, doe
continuallye warre againste them: but bycause we dyd
not vnderstande them well, wée coulde not perceyue how
farre it was to that Countrey. Our Captaine shewed
them redde Copper, whyche in theyr language they
call *Caignetadze*, and lokyng towarde that Countrey
wyth signes, asked them if anye came from thence,
they shakyng theyr heades annsweared no: but they
shewed vs that it came from *Saguenay*, and that lyeth
cleane contrarye to the other. After we hadde hearde
and séene these things of them, we drewe to oure boates
accompanyed wyth greate multitude of those people:
some of them when as they sawe anye of oure fellowes
wearye, they woulde take them vppe on theyr shoulders, and carrye them as on horsebacke. So soone as
we came to oure boates, we hoysed sayle to goe towarde
ouer Gallion, doubting of some mischaunce. Oure de-
parture grieued and displeased them verye muche,
for they followed vs along the Riuer as farre as they
coulde: wée wente so faste that on Mondaye beyng
the fourth of October wée came where oure Gallion was. The Tuesdaye followyng, being the fifthe
of the moneth, we hoysed sayle, and wyth oure Gallion and
boates.

boates, departed from thence toward the prouince of *Canada*,
to the port of the Holy Crosse, where we had left our ships.
The seauenth daye we came against a riuer that commeth
from the North, and entred into that riuer, at the entraunce
wherof are foure little Ilandes, ful of faire and goodly trées:
we named that riuer The riuer of Fouetz : But bycause one
of those Ilandes stretcheth himselfe a great way into the riuer, our Captaine at the point of it caused a goodlye greate
Crosse to be set vppe, and commaunded the boats to be made
readie, that with the nexte tide he mighte goe vp to the sayde
riuer, and consider the qualitie of it, whiche we did, and that
daye wente vp as farre as we coulde: but bycause we founde
it to bée of no importaunce, and that wée coulde sounde no
bottome, we retourned down and back againe.

¶ Howe wee came to the Port of the *Holie Crosse*, and in
    what state we founde our shippes: and howe the Lorde
    of the Countrey came to visite oure Captaine, and oure
    Captaine him: and of certaine particular customes of the
    people.   CHAP. 9.

VPon Monday being the eleuenth of October we came to
the Port of the Holy Crosse, where our shippes were, ⸿
founde that the maisters and Mariners we had lefte there,
had made and reared a Trench before the ships, altogither
closed with great péeces of Timber set vprighte and verye
well fastened togither: then had they beset the saide trenche
aboute with péeces of Artillerie and other necessarie things
to shielde and defende themselues from the power of all the
Countrey. So soone as the Lorde of the Countrey heard of
our comming, the next day being the twelfth of October, he
came to visit vs, accompanied with Taignoagny, Domagaia,
and many others, fayning to be verye glad of our comming,
making muche of our Captain, who as friendly as he could,
entertayned them, albeit they had not deserued it. Donnacona their Lord desired our Captaine the next day to come
                                                          and

and sée *Canada*, which he promised to do: for the next day being
the thirténth of the moneth, he with all his gentlemen, and
fiftie Mariners very wel appointed, went to visite Donnacona and his people, about a league from our ships. The place
where they make their abode, is called *Stadagona*. When we
were about a stones cast from their houses, manye of the inhabitours came to méete vs, being all set in a ranke, and (as
their custome is,) the men al on one side, and the wome on the
other, stil dauncing & singing without any ceasing: and after
we had saluted and receiued one another, our Captaine gaue
them kniues and such other slight things : then he caused all
the women and childrẽ to passe along before him, giuing
ech one a ring of Tin, for which they gaue him harty thãks:
that done, our Captaine was by Donnacona and Taignoagny, broughte to their houses (the qualitie considered) were
very well prouided, and stored with suche victualles as the
Countrey yéeldeth, to passe away the Winter withal. Then
they shewed vs the skinnes of fiue mens heades spred vpon
bourds as we do vse parchmẽt, Donnacona told vs that they
were skinnes of *Toudamani*, a people dwelling towarde the
South, who continually doe warre against them. Moreouer
they tolde vs, that it was two yeares paste that those *Toudamans* came to assault them, yea euen into the said riuer, in an
Iland that lyeth ouer against *Saguenay*, where they had bene
the night before, as they were going a warfaring in *Honguedo*, with two hundereth persons, men, women, and childrẽ,
who being all asléepe in a fort that they had made, they were
assaulted by the saide *Toudamans*, who put fire rounde aboute
the fort; and as they would haue come out of it to saue themselues, they were al slaine, onely fiue excepted, who escaped.
For which losse they yet sorrowed, shewing with signes, that
one day they woulde be reuenged: that done, we came to our
shippes againe.

R. ¶The

¶ The manner how the people of that Country liue: and of certaine conditions : of their Faith, manners, and cuſtomes. CHAP. 10.

This people beleeue no whit in God, but in one whõ they cal Cudruaigni: they ſay that often he ſpeaketh with thẽ and telleth them what weather ſhall followe, whether good oʒ badde. Moʒeouer they ſay, that when he is angrye wyth them hée caſteth duſte into theyʒ eyes : they beleeue that whẽ they die they go into the Stars, and thence by little and little deſcend downe into the *Horizon*, euen as the Stars doe, and ỹ then they go into cer taine gréene fieldes full of goodly faire & pʒetious trées, ſloures, and ſruites. After that they had giuen vs theſe things to vnderſtand, we ſhewed them their errour, and tolde that their Cudruaigni did but deceiue them, foʒ hée is but a Diuell and an euill ſpirite : aſſirming vnto them, that there is but one only God, who is in Heauen, and who giueth vs all neceſſaries, being the creatour of all himſelfe, and that onely we muſt belieue in him : moʒeouer, that it is neceſſarie foʒ vs to be baptiʒed, otherwiſe we are dampned into Hel. This and manye other things concerning our faith and religion we ſhewed them, all whiche they did eaſily belieue, calling their Cudruaigni, Agouiada: ſo that very erneſt-ly they deſired and pʒayed our Captaine that he woulde cauſe them to be baptiſed, and their Loʒde, Taignoagny, Doma-gaia, and all the people of the towne came vnto vs, hoping to be baptiſed : but bycauſe we did not thʒoughely knowe theyʒ minde, and that there was no bodie coulde giue them our beliefe and religion to vnderſtande, we excuſed our ſelues, deſiring Taignoagny and Domagaia to tell the reſte of theyʒ Countreymenne, that we woulde come againe ano-ther time, and bʒing Miniſters and Pʒieſtes with vs, foʒ without them they coulde not be baptiſed: whiche they dyd eaſilye belieue : foʒ Domagaia and Taignoagny hadde séene

manye

A noughtie liuer.

many children baptiſed in Bꝛytain whiles they were there. Whiche pꝛomiſe when they hearde, they ſeemed to be verie gladde. They liue in common togither, and of ſuch commodities as their Countrey yéeldeth they are indifferentlye well ſtoared, the inhabitours of the Towne of clOath themſelues with the ſkinnes of certaine wilde beaſts, but verie miſerably. In Winter they weare hoſen and ſhoes made of wilde beaſtes ſkinnes, and in Sommer they goe barefooted. They kéepe and obſerue the rytes of matrimony, ſauing that euerye one weddeth two oꝛ thꝛée wiues, whiche (theyꝛ huſbandes being deade) doe neuer marrye agayne, but foꝛ the deathe of theyꝛ huſbandes weare a certayne blacke wéede all the dayes of their life, beſmearing all their faces with cole duſte and greaſe mingled togyther almoſte halfe a quarter of an inche thicke, and by that they are knowen to be Widowes. They haue a filthye and deteſtable uſe in marrying of their maydens, and that is thys, they putte them all (after they are of lawfull age to marrie) in a common place, as harlots frée foꝛ euerie manne that will haue to doe wyth them, untill ſuch tyme as they finde a matche. Thys I ſaye, bycauſe I I haue ſéene by experience manye houſen full of thoſe Damoſels, euen as our ſcholes are full of childꝛen in *Fraunce* to learne to reade. Moꝛeouer, the miſrule and riot that they kéepe in thoſe houſes is verie greate, foꝛ verie wantonlye they ſpoꝛte and dallye togither, ſhewing whatſoeuer God hathe ſent them. They are no men of greate labour. They ploughe theyꝛ groundes with certain péeces of wood, as big as halfe a ſwoꝛde, on whiche grounde groweth theyꝛ coꝛne. The call it *Offici* it is as bigge as our ſmall Beaſon, there is great quantitie of it growing in *Breſil*. They haue alſo great ſtoꝛe of muſke Milions, Pompons, Gourdes, Cowcombers, Peaſon, and Beanes of euerye coloure, yet differing frō ours. There groweth alſo a certain kind of Herb, wherof in Sommer they make greate pꝛouiſion foꝛ all the yeare,

R.ij.   making

making great accompt of it, and only men vse of it, and firſt, they cauſe it to be dryed in the Sunne, then weare it aboute their necke wrapped in a little beaſtes ſkin made like a little bagge, with a hollow péece of ſtone oꝛ wood like a pipe:then when they pleaſe they make pouder of it , and then put it in one of the endes of the ſayd Coꝛnet oꝛ pipe, and laying a cole of fire vppon it, at the other ende ſucke ſo long , that they fill their bodies full of ſmoke, till that it commeth out of their mouth and noſtrils, euen as out of the Tonnel of a Chimny. They ſay that this doth kepe them warm and in health: they neuer go without ſome of it about thē . We our ſelues haue tryed the ſame ſmoke , and hauing put it in our mouthes, it ſéemed that they had filled it with Pepper duſt , it is ſo hote. The women of that Countrey doe labour muche moꝛe than the men, as well in fiſhing, (wherto they are greatly giuen,) as in tilling and husbanding theyꝛ groūds, and other things: as wel the mē as women, and childꝛen, are very much moꝛe able to reſiſt colde, than ſauage beaſtes, foꝛ we with our own eyes haue ſéene ſome of thē, when it was coldeſt, (which cold was extréeme raw, and bitter) come to our ſhips ſtark naked going vppon Snowe and Iſe, which thing ſéemeth incredible to them that haue not ſéene it. When as the Snowe and Iſe lyeth on the ground, they take great ſtoꝛe of wilde beaſts, as Faunes, Stagges, Beares, Martons, Hares, and Foxes, with diuerſe other ſoꝛtes, whoſe fleſhe they eate rawe, hauing firſte dꝛyed it in the Sunne oꝛ ſmoke , and ſo they doe their fiſhe. As farre foꝛth as we coulde perceiue and vnderſtande by theſe people, it were a very eaſie thing to bꝛing thē to ſome familiaritie and ciuilitie , and make them learne what one woulde. The Loꝛd GOD foꝛ his mercies ſake ſette therevnto his helping hande when hée ſéeth cauſe. Amen.

¶ Of the greatnesse and deapth of the sayd Riuer, and of
the sortes of Beastes, Birdes, Fishes, and other things that
we haue seene, with the scituation of the place. Cʜᴀ. ɪɪ.

THe sayd Riuer beginneth beyond the Ilano of _Thassump-
cion_, ouer against the high Mountaynes of _Honguedo_, and
of the seauen Ilands. The distance ouer from one side to the
other, is about 35. or 40. leagues. In the middest it is aboue
100. faddome deepe. The surest way to sayle vpon it, is on the
South side, and towarde the North, that is to say, from the
sayd seauen Ilandes, where from side to side, there is seauen
leagues, where are also two great Riuers that come downe
from the hilles of _Saguenay_, and make diuers very dangerous
shealues in the Sea. At the entrance of those two Riuers, we
saw many and great store of Whales, and sea Horses. Ouerthwart the sayd Ilands, there is another little Riuer that
runneth along those marrish groundes about three or foure
leagues, wherein there is great store of water fowles. From
the head of that Riuer to _Hochelaga_, there is about three hundred leagues: the originall beginning of it is in the riuer that
commeth from _Saguenay_, which riseth and springeth among
high and steepe hilles: it entreth into that Riuer before it commeth to the prouince of _Canada_ on the North side. That riuer
is very deepe, high, and straight, wherefore it is very dangerous for any vessell to goe vpon it. After that riuer, followeth
the prouince of _Canada_, wherein are many people dwelling in
open boroughes and villages. There are also in the circuite
and territorie of _Canada_, along, and within the sayd riuer, many other Ilands, some great, and some small, among whiche,
there is one that contepneth aboue tenne leagues in length,
full of goodly and high trees, and also many Uines. You may
go into it from both sides, but yet the surest passage is on the
South side. On the shoare or bancke of that Riuer West-
warde, there is a goodly, faire, and delectable sluce, or Creeke,
conuenient and fitte for to harborough Shippes. Hard by,
there is in that Riuer one place very narrow, deepe, and swift
running,

running, but it is not paſſing the third part of a league, ou:r
againſt the which, there is a goodly high péece of land, with a
Towne therein : and the Countrey about it is very well tilled and wroughte, and as good as poſſibly can bée ſéene. That
is the place and abode of Donnacona, and of our two men
we toke in our firſte voyage, it is called *Stadagona*. But befoze we come to it, there are foure other peopled Townes,
that is to ſay, *Ayraſte, Starnatan, Tailla*, whiche ſtandeth vppon a hill, and *Scitadin*, and then *Stadagona*, vnder whiche
Towne toward the Nozth, the Riuer and Pozte of the holy Croſſe is, where we ſtayd from the fiftenth of September,
vntill the ſirtéenth of May 1536. and there oure Shippes re-
mayned dzie, as we haue ſayde befoze. That place béeing
paſt, we found the habitation of the people called *Teguenon-
dahi*, ſtanding vpon an high Mountayne, and the valley of
Hochelay, whiche ſtandeth in a Champaigne Countrey. All
that Countrey is full of ſundzye ſortes of woode, and many Vynes, vnleſſe it be about the places that are inhabited,
where they haue pulled vp the Trées to till and laboure the
grounde, and to builde their Houſes and Lodgings. There
is greate ſtoze of Stagges, Déeres, Beares, and other
ſuche lyke ſortes of Beaſtes, as Connies, Hares, Martons, Foxes, Otters, Weaſels, Badgers, and Mice excée-
ding greate, and diuers other ſortes of Veniſon. They cloath
themſelues with the Skinnes of thoſe Beaſtes, bycauſe
they haue nothing elſe to make them apparell withall.
There are alſo many ſortes of Birds, as Cranes, Swannes,
Cignets, wild Géeſe white and gray, Duckes, Thzuſhes,
blacke Birdes, Turtles, wilde Pigeons, Lenites, Finches,
redde bzeaſtes, Stares, Nightingales, Sparrowes, and o-
ther Birdes, euen as in *France*. Alſo as we haue ſayde befoze,
the ſayde Riuer is the plentifulleſt of Fiſh that euer hath of
any man bin ſéene oz heard of, bycauſe that from the head to
the end of it, accozding to their ſeaſons, you ſhall find all ſorts
of freſh water fiſh, and ſalt. There are alſo many Whales,
Pozpoiſes, Seahozſes, and Adhothuis, whiche is a kinde of

Fiſh

fiſh that we had neuer ſéene nor heard of befoze. They are
as great as Pozpoiſes, as white as any Snow, their bodys
and head faſhioned as a gray hound, they are woont alwayes
to abide betwéene the freſh and ſalt water, which beginneth
betwéene the Riuer of *Saguenay* and *Canada*.

¶ Of certayne aduertiſements and notes giuen vnto vs by
thoſe Countreymen, after our returne from *Hochelaga*.
CHAP. 12.

Fter our returne from *Hochelaga*, we haue dealte, traf-
fickt, and with great familiaritie and loue haue bin con-
uerſant with thoſe that dwelt néereſt vnto our Shippes, excepte that ſometimes we had ſtrife and contention with certayne naughtie people, full ſoze againſte the will of the o-
thers. We vnderſtode of Donnacona, and of others, that
the ſayde Riuer is called *Saguenays* Riuer, and goeth to *Sa-*
guenay, béeing ſomewhat moze than a league farther Weaſt
Pozth-weaſt, and that eyght oz nyne dayes iourneys beyond, it will beare but ſmall Boates. But the right and
readye way to *Saguenay*, is from that Riuer to *Hochelaga*,
and then into another that commeth from *Saguenay*, and then
entreth into the fozeſayde Riuer, and that there is yet one
moneths ſayling thither. Mozeouer, they tolde vs, and gaue
vs to vnderſtande, that there are people clad with cloth as we
are, very honeſt, and many inhabited Townes, and that they
haue great ſioze of Golde, and redde Copper, and that aboute
the land the ſayd firſt Riuer to *Hochelaga* and *Saguenay*, is an
Iland enuironed rounde about with that and other Riuers,
which beyond *Saguenay* enter into two oz thzée great Lakes,
and that there is a Sea of freſh water found, and as they
haue heard ſay of thoſe of *Saguenay*, there was neuer manne
heard of that founde out the way and end thereof: foz as they
tolde vs, they themſelues were neuer there. Mozeouer,
they tolde vs, that where we had lefte oure Galion when
we

we wente to *Hochelaga*, there is a Riuer that goeth South-weast, from whence there is a whole moneths sayling to goe to a certayne lande, where there is nepther Yse nor Snow séene, where the inhabitours do cōtinually warre one against another, where is great store of Oranges, Almonds, Nuttes, and Apples, with many other sortes of fruites, and that the men and women are cladde with Beastes Skinnes euen as they: we asked them if there were any Gold or red Copper, they answered no. I take this place to be toward *Florida*, as farre as I could perceyue and vnderstand by their signes and tokens.

¶ Of a ſtrange and cruell diſeaſe that came to the people of *Stadagona*, wherwith bycauſe we did haunt their company, we wer ſo infected, that there died 25.of our companye. CHAP. 13.

IN the moneth of December, we vnderstode that the Plague or Pestilence was come to the people of *Stadago-na*, in such sort, that before we knew of it, accordyng to their confession, there were dead aboue 50. wherevpon we forbad them nepther to come néere our Forte, nor about our Ships, or vs. And albeit we had driuen them from vs, the sayd vnknowen sicknesse beganne to spread it selfe amongst vs, after the strangest sort that euer was eyther heard of or séene, in so much, as some did lose all their strength, and could not stand on their féete, then did theyr legges swell, their sinnowes shrinke as blacke as any cole. To others, all their Skinnes was spotted with spottes of bloud of a purple couloure: then did it ascende vp alofte to theyr anckles, knées, thighes, shoulders, armes, and necke: their mouth became stincking, their gummes so rotten, that all the flesh did fall off, euen to the rootes of the Téeth, which did also almost all fall out. With such infection did this Sicknesse spreade it selfe in oure thrée Shippes, that aboute the middle of Febzuary, of a hundreth and tenne persons that we were, there were

not

not tenne whole, so that one coulde not helpe the other, a
moste horrible and pitifull case, considering the place wée
were in, forsomuch as the people of the Country would day-
ly come before our forte, and saw but few of vs. There were
alreadie eight deade, and more than fiftie sicke, and as wée
thought, past al hope of recouerie. Our Captaine séeing this
our misery, and that the sicknesse was gone so far, ordained
and commaunded, that euery one shoulde deuoutly prepare
himselfe to prayer, and in remembraunce of Christ, caused
his Image to be sette vp vpon a trée, aboute a Flight shotte
from the forte, amidst the Ice and Snowe, giuing all men
to vnderstande, that on the Sonday following, seruice should
be saide there, and, that whosoeuer coulde goe, sicke, or whole,
should go thither in Procession, singing the seauen Psalmes
of Dauid, with other Letanies, praying moste hartily, that
it woulde please the said our Christ to haue compassion vpon
vs. Seruice beyng done, and as well celebrated as we could,
our Captaine there made a vowe, that if it woulde please
God to giue him leaue to returne into *Fraunce*, he would goe
on pilgrimage to our Lady of *Rocquemado*. That daye Phi-
lip Rougemont, borne in *Amboisa*, died, being two and twenty yeares olde, and bicause the sicknes was to vs vnknowen,
our Capitaine caused him to be ripped, to sée if by any means
possible we might know what it was, and so séeke means to
saue and preserue the reste of the company: he was founde to
haue his heart white, but rotten, & more than a pottle of red
water about it: his liuer was indifferent faire, but his lungs
blacke and mortified, his bloud was altogither shruke about
the heart, so that when he was opened, great quantity of rotten bloud issued out from aboute his heart: his milt toward
the backe was somwhat perished, rough as if it had bin rub-
bed against a stone. Moreouer, bicause one of his thighs was
very black without, it was opened, but within it was whole
and sounde: that done, as wel as we could he was buryed. In
suche sorte did the sicknes continue and encrease, that there
were not aboue thrée sound men in the ships, and none was
able

L.

able to go vnder hatches to draw drinke for himselfe, nor for his fellowes. Sometimes we were conſtrayned to burie ſome of the dead vnder the Snowe, bycauſe we were not able to digge any graues for them, the ground was ſo hard froſen, and we ſo weake. Beſides this, we did greately feare, that the people of the Countrey would perceyue our weakeneſſe and miſerie, whiche to hide, our Captayne, whome it pleaſed God alwayes to keepe in health, woulde go out with two or three of the companye, ſome ſicke, and ſome whole, whome when he ſaw out of the Fort, he would throw ſtones at them and chide them, faigning, that ſo ſoone as he came againe, he woulde beate them, and then with ſignes ſhew the people of the Countrey, that he cauſed all his men to worke and laboure in the Shippes, ſome in mending them, ſome in beating of chalke, ſome in one thing, and ſome in another, and that he woulde not haue them come forthe, till their worke was done. And to make his tale ſeeme true and likely, he woulde make all his men whole and ſound to make a great noyſe, with knocking ſtickes, ſtones, hammers, and other things togither, at which time, we were ſo oppreſſed, and greeued with that ſickneſſe, that we had loſt all hope euer to ſee France agayne, if God of his infinite goodneſſe and mercie had not with his pitifull eye looked vpon vs, and reuealed a ſingular and excellent remedie againſt all diſeaſes vnto vs, the beſt that euer was founde vpon earth, as heereafter ſhall followe.

¶ How long we ſtayed in the Porte of the holy Croſſe amidſt the Snow and Yſe, and how many dyed of the ſaid diſeaſe, from the beginning of it, to the midſt of March. CHAP. 14.

FRom the midſt of Nouember, vntill the midſt of Aprill, we were kepte in amidſt the Yſe aboue one faddome thicke, and Snow aboue foure foote high, and more higher than the ſides of our Shippes, which laſted till that time, in

                                                                    ſuch

such sorte, that all our drinckes were frosen in the Uessels, and the Yse through all the Shippes, was aboue a hande-breadth thicke, as well aboue hatches as beneath, and so much of the Riuer as was fresh, vntill to *Hochelaga*, was frosen, in which space there dyed fiue and twentie of our best and chiefest men, and all the rest so sicke, that we thoughte they shoulde neuer recouer agayne, onely three or foure ex-cepted. Then it pleased God to cast his pitifull eye vpon vs, and sente vs the knowledge and remedie of our healthes and recouerie, in such maner as in the next Chapter shall be shewed.

¶ How by the grace of God we had notice of a certayne tree, wherby we all recouered our health: and the maner how to vse it. CHAP. 15.

Our Captayne considering oure estate (and how that sicknesse was encreased and hote amongst vs) one daye wente foorth of the Forte, and walking along vppon the Yse, he saw a troupe of those Countreymen comming from *Sta-dacona*, among whiche was Domagaia, who not passing tenne or twelue dayes afore, had bene very sicke with that disease, and had his knees swolne as bigge as a Child of two yeares olde, all his sinowes shruncke togither, hys teeth spoyled, his gummes rotten, and stincking. Oure Captayne seeing him whole and sound, was thereat maruellous glad, hoping to vnderstand and knowe of him how he had healed himselfe, to the ende he might ease and help his men. So soone as they were come neere him, he asked Domagaia how he had done to heale hymselfe, he answered, that he had take the iuice and sappe of the leaues of a certayne Tree, and therewith had healed himselfe: For it was a singular remedie agaynst that disease. Then our Captayne asked of hym if any were to bee had thereabout, desiring him to shew it him, for to heale a ser-uant of his, who whilest he was in *Canada* with Donnacona, &

was stricken with that disease: That he did, bicause he would
not shewe the number of his sicke men . Domagaia straight
sent two women to fetche some of it, whyche broughte tenne
or twelue braunches of it , and therewithall shewed vs the
way howe to vse it, and that is thus, to take the barke and
leaues of the saide trée, and boile it togither, then to drinke of
the saide decoction one daye , and the other not , and the
dregges of it to be put vpon his legs that is sicke: moreouer,
they told vs , ŷ the vertue of that trée was, to heale any other
disease : the trée is in their language called AMEDA . Our
Captaine presently caused some of that drinke to be made for
his men to drinke of it, but there was none durste taste of it,
excepte one or two, who ventured the drinking of it, onely
to taste and proue it: the other séeyng that, did the like ; and
presently recouered their health , and were delyuered of
that sickenesse, and what other disease soeuer , in suche
sorte, that there were some hadde béene diseased and troubled wyth the French Pockes foure or fiue yeares , and
wyth thys drinke were cleane healed . After thys medi-
cine was founde and proued to be true , there was suche
strife aboute it , who shoulde be firste to take of it , that
they were readye to kill one another, that a trée as bigge
as anye Oake in *Fraunce* , was spoyled and lapped bare ,
and occupyed all in fiue or sixe dayes, and wroughte so
well, that if all the Phisitions of *Mountpelier*, and of *Louaine*,
hadde béene there wyth all the drugges of *Alexandria*,
they woulde not haue done so muche in one yeare , as that
trée dydde in sixe dayes, and didde so preuaile, that as manye as vsed of it, by the grace of G O D recouered their
health.

Howe

¶ Howe the Lorde *Donnacona* accompanyed with *Taigno-agny* and dyuers others, fayning that they woulde goe to hunt Stags, and other wilde Deere, taryed out twoo moneths, and at theyr returne broughte a greate multitude of people with them, that we were not wont to see before. CHAP. 16.

Hileſt that diſeaſe laſted in our ſhips, the Loꝛd Donnacona, Taignoagny, with many others, fayning, that they would go catch Stags and Deere, which is in their tongue called *Aiouneſta*, and *Aſquenoudo*, bycauſe the Ice and Snow was not ſo bꝛoken along the riuer that they coulde ſaile, it was tolde vs of Domagaia, and others, that they woulde ſtay out but foꝛtnight, and we beléued it, but they ſtayed aboue two moneths, whych made vs miſtruſt that they had bin gone to raiſe the Country to come againſte vs, and doe vs ſome diſpleaſure, wée ſéyng oure ſelues ſo weake and faint. Albeit we had vſed ſuch diligence and pollicie in oure Foꝛte, that if all the power of the country had bin aboute it, they coulde haue done nothyng but looke vpon vs: and whyleſt they were foꝛthe, manye of the people came daylye to our ſhippes, and bꝛought vs freſh meate, as Stags, Deeres, Fiſhes, with diuers other things, but helde them at ſuche an erceſſiue pꝛice, that rather than they would ſell them anye thing cheape, many times they woulde carry them backe againe, bycauſe that yeare the Winter was very long ⁊ they had ſome ſcarcitie and néede of them.

¶ How *Donnacona* came to *Stadagona* againe with a greate number of people, and bycauſe he would not come to viſite our Captaine, fayned himſelfe to be ſore ſicke, whiche he did onely to haue the Captaine come and ſee him. CHAP. 17.

N the one and twentith of Apꝛill Domagaia came to the ſhoare ſide, accompanyed with dyuers luſty and ſtrong

men

men, such as we were not wont to sée, and tolde vs that their Lord Donnacona woulde the next daye come and sée vs, and bring great store of Déers fleshe, and other things with him. The next day he came and brought a greate number of men in *Stadagona*, to what end, and for what cause we knew not, but (as the prouerb saith) he that takes héede and shields him selfe from all men, maye happe to scape from some, for wée had néed to looke about vs, considering how in number we were diminished, and in strength greatlye weakened, long of our sicknesse we had bene troubled withall, that we were constrayned to leaue one of our shippes in the sayde Port of the Holy Crosse. Our Captain was warned of their comming, and how they had brought a great number of mé with them, for Domagaia came to tel it vs, and durst not passe the riuer that was betwixt *Stadagona* and vs, as he was wonte to doe, wherevpon we mistrusted of some treason. Our Captain séeing this, sent one of his seruantes to them, accompanied with Iohn Poulet being best beloued of those people, to sée who were there, and what they dyd. The sayde Poulet and the other faygned onely to be come to visite Donnacona, and bryng him certaine presentes, bycause they hadde bene togither a good while in the sayde Donnaconas Towne. So soone as he hearde of their comming, he gotte hymselfe to bedde, fayning to be verye sicke. That done, they wente to Taignoagny hys house to sée him, and wheresoeuer they wente, they sawe so manye people, that in a manner one coulde not styrre for an other, and suche menne as they were neuer wonte to sée. Taignoagny would not permitte oure menne to enter in anye other housen, but styll kepte them companye, and broughte them halfe way to our ships, and tolde that if it would please our Capitaine to shewe him so muche fauoure as to take a Lord of the Country people, whose name Agonna, of whom he hadde receyued some displeasure, and carrye hym wyth

hym

hym into *Fraunce*, he shoulde therefore for euer be bounde vnto hym, and woulde doe for hym whatsoeuer he coulde possible, and would do for him whatsoeuer he woulde commaund
him, and bade the seruaunt to come againe the nexte daye,
and bryng an aunsweare. Oure Capitayne béeyng aduertised of so manye people that were there, not kno-
wyng to what ende, purposed to playe a pretty prancke,
that is to saye, to take theyr Lorde Donnacona, Taignoagny, Domagaia, and some more of the chiefest of them, prisoners, in so muche as before he had purposed, to bring them
into *Fraunce*, to shewe vnto our King what he hadde séene
in those Westerne partes, and maruailes of the worlde, for
that Donnacona had tolde vs, that he hée hadde béene in the
Countrey of *Saguenay*, in whych are infinite Rubies, Golde,
and other riches, and that there are white menne, who
clothe themselues wyth wollen cloth euen as wée doe in
Fraunce. The sayde Lorde was an olde manne, and
euen from hys chyldehœde hadde neuer lefte off nor cea-
sed from trauayling into straunge Countreys, as well
by Seas and Ryuers, as by Lande. The sayde Powlet,
and the other hauing tolde oure Capitayne theyr Embas-
sage, and shewed hym what Taignoagny hys wyll
was, the nexte daye hée sente hys seruaunt agayne, to
bidde Taignoagny come and sée hym, and shewe what
hée woulde, for hée shoulde bée verye well entertayned,
and also parte of hys wyll shoulde bée accomplyshed.
Taignoagny sente hym worde, that the nexte daye hée
woulde come and bryng the Lorde Donnacona wyth
hym, and hym that hadde so offended hym, whyche hée
dydde not, but stayed two dayes, in whyche tyme none
came from *Stadagona* to oure Shyppes, as they were wont
to doe, but rather fledde from vs, as if wée woulde haue
slayne them, so that then wée playnely percevued theyr
knauery.

But

But when they vnderſtwde, that thoſe of *Sidatin* dɩd frequent
our company,and that we had foꝛſaken the bottome of a ſhip
whyche we woulde leaue,to haue the olde nailes oute of it,
the thirde daye followyng they came from *Stadagona*, and
moſte of them wythout difficultie dɩd paſſe from one ſɩde of
the riuer to the other with ſmall Skɩffes : but Donnacona
hæ̀ woulde not come ouer, Taignoagny and Domagaia ſtꝏd
talking togither aboue an houre befoꝛe they woulde come o-
uer, at laſte they came to ſpeake with our Captaine. There
Taignoagny pꝛayed him that he woulde cauſe the foꝛeſayde
man to be taken and carryed into *Fraunce*. Oure Captaine
refuſed to doe it , ſaying, that his Kyng had foꝛbɩdden hym
to bꝛing any man oꝛ woman into *Fraunce*,only that he might
bꝛing two oꝛ thꝛæ̀ yong boyes to learne the language, but
that he woulde willingly carry hym to another lande , and
there putte hym. Our Captaine ſpake this, onely to aſſure
them, that they ſhould bꝛing Donnacona wyth them, whom
they had lefte on the other ſɩde, whych woꝛdes, when Taignoagny hearde,he was very glad,thinking he ſhoulde neuer
retourne into *Fraunce* againe, and therefoꝛe pꝛomiſed to
come the nexte daye,whych was the day of the holy Croſſe,
and woulde bꝛyng Donnacona and all the people wyth
hym.

¶ Howe that vpon Holyroode day our Captaine cauſed
    a Croſſe to be ſet vp in our Forte : and howe the Lord
    Donnacona, Taignoagny, Domagaia, and others of theyr
    company came : and of the taking of the ſaide Lorde.
    CHAP. 18.

The thirde of May beyng Holy rꝏde day, our Captaine
foꝛ the ſolemnitie of the daye,cauſed a gꝏdly faire croſſe
of thirtie fꝏte in heigth to be ſette vppe, vnder the croſſet of
which he cauſed a ſhielde to be hanged , wherein was the
Armes of *Fraunce* , and ouer them was wꝛitten in antique
                        letters :

letters: FRANCISCVS PRIMVS DEI GRATIA FRANCORVM REX REGNAT, and vpon that daye, about none, there came a great number of the people of *Stadagona*, Men, Women, and Children, who told vs, that their Lord Donnacona, Taignoagny, and Domagaia, were comming, whereof we were very glad, hoping to retayne them. Aboute two of the Clocke in the after noone they came, and being come neere our Shippes, our Captayne went to salute Donnacona, who also shewed him a merrie countenance, albeit very fearefully his eye were still bent toward the woode. Shortly after came Taignoagny, who bade Donnacona, that he should not enter in our Forte, and therefore fire was brought forth by one of our men, and kindled where their Lord was. Our Captayne prayed him to come into our Ships to eate and drinke as he was wont to do, and also Taignoagny, who promised, that after a while he would come, and so they did, and entred in our Shippes: but first it was tolde our Captayne by Domagaia, that Taignoagny had spoken yll of him, and that he had bid Donnacona he should not come aboard our Shippes. Our Captayne perceyuing that, came out of the Forte, and saw that onely by Taignoagny his warning, the Women ranne away, and none but men stayed in great number, wherefore he straight commanded his men to lay hold on Donnacona, Taignoagny, and Domagaia, and two more of the chiefest, whome he poynted vnto: then he commanded them to make the other to retire. Presently after, the Lord entred into the Forte with the Captayne, but by and by Taignoagny came to make him come out agayne. Our Captayne seeing that there was no other remedie, beganne to call vnto them to take them, to whose crye and voyce all his men came forth, and tooke the sayd Lord with the others, whome they had appoynted to take. The *Canadians* seeing their Lord taken, beganne to runne away, euen as Sheepe before the Woolfe, some crossing ouer the Riuer, some through the Woodes, each one seeking for his own aduantage. That done, we retired our selues, & laid vp the prisoners vnder good gard & safety.

M.

¶ How

¶ How the saide *Canadians* the night following came before our Ships to seeke their men, crying and howling al night like Wolues : of the talke and conclusion they agreed vpon the next day : and of the giftes which they gaue our Captaine. Chap. 19.

The night following, they came before our Shippes, (the Riuer being betwixte vs) striking their breastes, crying and howling like Wolues, still calling Agouhanna, thinking to speake with him, which oure Captayne for that time would not permitte, neyther all the next day till noone, wherevpon they made signes vnto vs, that we had hanged or killed hym. Aboute noone, there came as great a number in a cluster, as euer we saw, who wente to hide themselues in the Forest, excepted some, who with a loude voyce woulde call and crye to Donnacona to speake vnto them. Our Captayne then commanded Donnacona to be broughte vp on high to speake vnto them, and bade hym be merrie, for after he had spoken, and shewed vnto the King of *France* what he had seene in *Saguenay* and other Countreys, after tenne or twelue monethes, he shoulde returne againe, and that the King of *France* would giue him greate rewardes, whereat Donnacona was very glad, and speaking to the others, tolde it them, who in token of ioy, gaue out three great cryes, and then Donnacona and his people had great talke togither, whiche for wante of interpretours, can not be described. Oure Captayne bade Donnacona, that he shoulde cause them to come to the other side of the Riuer, to the ende they might better talke togither without any feare, and that he shoulde assure them, whiche Donnacona did, and there came a Boate full of the chiefest of them to the Shippes, and there anew beganne to talke togither, giuing greate prayse vnto our Captayne, and gaue him a presente of foure

and

and twentie chaynes of *Esurgny*, for that is the greateſt, and pretiouſeſt riches they haue in this worlde, for that they eſteeme more of that, than of any Golde or Siluer. After they hadde long talked togyther, and that theyr Lorde ſaw that there was no remedie to auoyde hys goyng into *Franca*, hee commaunded hys people the nexte daye, to bring him ſome victualles to ſerue hym by the way. Oure Captayne gaue Donnacona as a greate preſente, two frying pannes of Copper, eyght Hatchets, and other ſmall trifles, as kniues, and Beades, whereof hee ſeemed to bee very glad, who ſente them to his Wiues and Childzen. Likewiſe, he gaue certaine ſmall giftes to them that came to ſpeake with Donnacona, they thanked him greatly for them, and then wente to their Lodgings.

¶ How that the nexte daye, beeing the fifth of May, the ſayde people came agayne to ſpeake vnto theyr Lorde, and howe that foure Women came to the Shoare to bring him Victualles. Chap. 20.

Vpon the fifth of May, verye earelye in the Morning, a greate number of the ſayde people came agayne to ſpeake vnto theyr Lorde, and ſente a Boate, whyche in theyr tongue they call Caſnoui, wherein were only foure Women, without any manne for feare theyr menne ſhould be retayned.

Theſe Women brought great ſtore of victualles, as Millet, whyche is their Corne that they liue withall, Fleſhe, Fiſhe, and other thynges after theyr faſhion.

Theſe Women beeing come to our Shippes, our Captayne dyd very friendly entertayne them. Then Donnacona prayde our Captayne to tel thoſe women that he ſhould come agayne after ten or twelue monethes, & bring Donnacona to

M.ij. *Canada*

Canada agayne with him, that hee did only to appease them, which our Captayne did:wherefore the Women, as well by words as signes, seeme to be very glad, giuing our Captaine thankes, and tolde him, if he came againe,and brought Donnacona with him,they would giue him many things : in signe whereof, eache one gaue our Captayne a chayne of Esurgny, and then passed to the other side of the Riuer agayne, where stode all the people of Stadagona,who taking all leaue of their Lord, wente home agayne. On Saturday following, béeing the sixth of the moneth,we departed out of the sayd Porte, and came to harborough a little beneath the Ilande of Orleans, aboute twelue leagues from the Porte of the Holy Crosse, and vppon Sunday we came to the Iland of Filberdes, where we stayde vntill the sixtéenth of that Moneth, till the fiercenesse of the waters were past,which at that time ranne too swifte a course, and were too dangerous to come downe alongst the Riuer, and therefore we stayde till fayre weather came. In the meane while, many of Donnaconas Subiects came from the Riuer of Saguenay to him, but béeing by Domagaia aduertised, that their Lorde was taken to be caryed into France, they were all amazed, yet for all that, they would not leaue to come to oure Shippes, to speake to Donnacona, who tolde them, that after twelue moncthes, he shoulde come agayne, and that he shoulde be very well vsed, with the Captayne,Gentlemen, and Mariners.Which when they hearde, they greatly thanked oure Captayne, and gaue their Lorde thrée bundles of Beauers, and Sea Woolues Skinnes, with a greate knife of redde Copper that comnieth from Saguenay, and manye other thyngs. They gaue also to our Captayne a Chayne of Esurgny, for whyche oure Captayne gaue them tenne or twelue Hatchettes, and they gaue hym hartie thankes , and were very well contented . The nexte daye, béeing the sixtéenth of May, wée hoysed Sayle, and came from the sayde Iland of Fil burdes, to another, aboute fiftéene leagues from it, which is aboute fiue leagues in length , and there, to the ende

we

we might take some rest the night following, we staide that day, in hope the next day we might passe and auoyde the dangers of the riuer of *Saguenay*, which are great. That euening we went a land and found great store of Hares, of which we toke a great many, and therefore we called it The Ilande of Hares: in the night there arose a contrarie winde, with suche stormes and tempest, that we were constrayned to bende to the Iland of Filburdes againe, from whence we were come, bycause there was none other passage among the said Ilāds, and there we stayde till the one and twentie of that moneth, that faire weather and good winde came again: and then we sayled again, and that so prosperously, that we passed to *Honguedo*, which passage vntil that time had not bene discouered: we caused our ships to course athwart Pratos Cape, which is the beginning of the Port of *Cator*: and bicause the wind was good and conuenient, we sayled all day and all night without staying, and the next day we came to the middle of Brions Ilande, which we were not minded to do, to the end we might shorten our way. These two Ilands lie Northwest, & Southeast, and are about fiftie leagues one from another. The said Iland is in latitude 47. degrées and a halfe. Upon Thursday being the 26. of the moneth, and the feast of the Ascension of our Lord, we coasted ouer to go to a land and shallow of low sands, which are about eight leagues Sowthwest frō Brions Iland, on which are large Champaines, full of trées & towns, and also an enclosed sea, of which neyther could we sée or perceiue any gap, or any way to enter therein. On Friday following, being the 27. of the moneth, bycause the winde did change on the cost, we came to Brions Iland againe, where we stayed till the beginning of June, and toward the Southeast of this Iland, we sawe a land, séeming vnto vs as an Ilande, we coasted it about two leagues and a halfe, and by ye way we had notice of thrée other high Ilands, lying toward the Sandes, after we had known these things we retourned to the Cape of the saide land, whiche doeth diuide it selfe into two or thrée very high Capes: the waters ther are very déep,

M. iij.   and

& the floud of the Sea runneth so swift, that it cannot possibly
be swifter. That day we came to S. Laurence his Cape , whiche is 45. degrées and halfe towards the South, wée named
it S.Paules Cape, it is at 47. degrées, and a quarter . The
Sonday followyng, beyng the fourth of June and Whitsonday, we hadde notice of the coaste lying East Southeast,
distant from the new founde land aboute 22.leagues: and bycause the wind was against vs, we went to a Hauen, which
we named S.Spiritus Porte, where wée stayed till Tuisdaye
that we departed thence, sayling along that coaste vntill wée
came to S.Peters Ilandes. We found along the saide coaste
many very dangerous Ilands and Shelues, whych lye all in
the waye East southeast, and Weast Northweast about 23.
leagues into the Sea. Whilest we were in the said S.Peters
Ilands we met with many ships of *France* and of *Britaine*, we
stayed there from S. Barnabas day, being the 11.of the monrth, vntil the 16.that we departed thence and came to cape
of *Ras*, and entred into a Porte called *Rogaoso*, where we toke
in freshwater, and wood to passe the sea : there we lefte one
of our boates . Then vpon Monday, beyng the 19. of June,
we went from that Porte , and wyth suche good and prosperous weather we sailed along the Sea, in such sorte, that vpon the 6. of June. 1536. we came to the Porte of *S.Malo*, by
the grace of God, to whom we pray, here ending oure Nauigation, that of his infinite mercie he will graunte vs hys
grace and fauoure, and in the end, bring vs to the place of euerlasting felicitie.   A M E N.

Here foloweth the language of the Country, and Kingdomes
of *Hochelaga* and *Canada*, of vs called *Newe Fraunce*:
But firste the names of theyr Numbers.

Secada.	1	*Indahir.*	6
Tigneni.	2	*Aiaga.*	7
Hasche.	3	*Addigue.*	8
Hannaion.	4	*Madellon,*	9
Ouiscon.	5	*Assem.*	10